RABBIT HOLE

A Satanic Ritual Abuse
Survivor's Story

DAVID SHURTER

CONSIDER IT
CREATIVE

Council Bluffs, Iowa

ISBN13: 978-0-9848937-1-3
Library of Congress Control Number: 2011944437

Consider it Creative LLC
PO Box 113
Council Bluffs, IA 51502

DavidShurter.com
Facebook.com/DavidShurter

Brands and trademarks mentioned in the text of this book are property of their respective owners.

Photographs are from the private collection of David Shurter.

[Author's Note: I have changed the name of my last living sister and masked the names of a few other people who are denoted here by first name only. All other names and places are accurate.]

[Editor's Note: The editorial team decided, with the approval of the author, to add clarification of some of the people and events the author discusses in telling his story. These are denoted in separate sidebars within the text. We felt this background was important for readers who were not present during the time these events unfolded. These in-text explanations were added solely by the editors and are expressed through the actual newspaper headlines of the day, from scholarly studies on satanic ritual abuse, and from other authoritative sources, unless otherwise noted.]

Printed in the United States of America

10 9 8 7 6 5 4 3 2 1

CONTENTS

To Krutz and Macen, two of my "brothers" who are no longer with us on this side, but both of whom had an amazing impact on my life and outlook. Two of my dearest friends, I miss your laughter, and I am honored that you guys considered me a friend!

FOREWORD
JAMES RANDALL NOBLITT, PhD

Some of us are skeptics. We tend to disbelieve many things we see and hear. I was such a person about ritual abuse. Until I discovered otherwise in my psychological therapy practice. During the course of therapy, one of my patients told me narratives about having been abused in satanic rituals during her childhood. My wife and co-author, Pam Perskin Noblitt, and I wrote about this patient in our book, *Cult and Ritual Abuse: Its History, Anthropology and Recent Discovery in Contemporary America*, published by Praeger. With the passage of time I heard similar ritual abuse narratives from well over three hundred individuals. I am no longer a skeptic.

The psychological community now recognizes the diagnoses we are seeing in abused patients. At the same time, new organizations and individuals have come forward to reinterpret the recent upsurge in child abuse allegations as being so called false memories. Not all these memories are false. Many of them are real, and they are substantiated with other facts.

The weight of evidence indicates that childhood sexual abuse is underreported, not overstated. Nevertheless, this backlash continues to attract media coverage sometimes adversely affecting public policy and the outcomes of court hearings. Consequently abuse survivors are often not believed and then further betrayed by the society that failed to protect them in the first place.

In this kind of environment survivors of child abuse may be vulnerable to further abuse and exploitation because of the wide net of disbelief that has been cast. Therapists are cautious about accepting abuse survivors for treatment or in carefully considering child abuse as a possible explanation for their problems. This is sometimes true even though addressing abuse is essential to effectively treat these survivors.

Unfortunately, therapists sometimes fear that if their clients make claims that they were abused in childhood that the therapist may be blamed for these revelations. There have been numerous claims alleging the therapists "implanted" such memories of abuse. Civil lawsuits and complaints to licensing boards have been initiated even when the therapist did nothing wrong. Mental health professionals are often aware that they expose themselves to peril when they responsibly address child abuse histories.

The subject of ritual abuse further complicates the already complex and frequently misunderstood subject of child abuse. Some skeptical authors have claimed that there have never been any convictions for ritualistic crimes, or that the FBI has never found any evidence of ritual abuse, or that allegations of ritual abuse have only appeared in the U.S. These statements are incorrect, but nevertheless are frequently repeated by those who either have not investigated the subject carefully, or have not reported the facts accurately. We have written about these misstatements in our book, *Cult and Ritual Abuse.*

So what is ritual abuse? The short answer is abuse in a ritual, but it is really more than that. Ritual abuse consists of systematic, painful, terrifying, and humiliating acts that are typically initiated with young children—primarily before the age of two. These abuses are so profoundly disturbing that the child experiences psychological states of shock that include a sense of disconnection from the traumatic events.

As particular abusive rituals are methodically repeated, the child learns to undergo increasingly deeper states of dissociation of consciousness, or trancelike states. In other words, the trauma survivor is typically trained "to become another person." This is how dissociation of identity is learned. Memories are pushed further away and deeper in the mind—only to emerge much later in life.

Over time many survivors of extreme abuse end up with an inner world that might include such things as buildings, caves, or forests and groups of disconnected "parts" that may be perceived as inner "people" of all ages and of both genders, including also spirits, angels, demons, gods, animals, robots, and mythological characters—many of whom have specific assigned jobs to protect or save the abused survivor. This kind of trauma-based learning is sometimes called programming.

David Shurter takes you down his own personal "rabbit hole" and shares his survivor story in this book. He does not elaborate on all the unspeakable details of his abuse experiences. Instead, he focuses on his own interpersonal experiences in the context of Omaha subcultures that so far have been suspected but unknown and hidden from view. He addresses the abuses

3

of power that are often associated with the abuse of vulnerable people like David himself. I will not summarize his story for you; for that you will have to read it yourself.

James Randall Noblitt, PhD
Alliant International University
Alhambra, California
December 2011

INTRODUCTION

My parents, before I was even a gleam in their eyes, became involved with some very warped individuals who worshiped the Devil and enacted horrible rites in a practicing satanic coven. Associated with some rich and well-connected members of Omaha's elite, the events that occurred are far from fantasy, and if the true story and the surprising participants were ever revealed, a dark cloud of suspicion would shroud Omaha, Nebraska, ensnaring a political system in its web—in an undercover conspiracy that extends to the White House.

This book is, finally, the story of what was honestly going on in Omaha until the late 1980s, when all hell broke loose.

Rumors and conjecture still surface in Omaha about a time in the mid-1980s when a group of rich men drove a local bank called the Franklin Credit Union into the ground. Books like *The Franklin Cover-Up: Child Abuse, Satanism, and Murder in Nebraska* by State Senator John Decamp (1996) and *The Franklin Scandal: A Story of Powerbrokers, Child Abuse & Betrayal* by Nick Bryant (2009) have recounted details of a pedophile ring that was based in Omaha but reached all the way to the White House.

Among other crimes, the secret but powerful members of the group managed to swindle Franklin Credit Union out of nearly $40 million. The British documentary *Conspiracy of Silence,* detailing many of the concerns at the time, was scheduled to be aired on the Discovery Channel on May 3, 1994, according to *TV Guide* magazine, but the show was cancelled at the last minute, due to pressure by influential members of Congress. Thanks to YouTube and the Internet, however, the documentary can now be viewed by the whole world.

Concerning the Satanism that was being practiced, Omaha's local Offutt Air Force Base, headquarters of the U.S. Strategic Air Command and underground bunker command in the event of nuclear war, was believed to be somehow involved, as was the MK-ULTRA mind control project. Beginning in the Cold War 1950s, this program had a plethora of projects dedicated to opening the frontiers of trauma-based mind control. That is, the American government through the CIA used drugs, hypnosis, and torture to break the mind into compartments that could then be controlled (think Gitmo and waterboarding here). The story told to those Congressional representatives who were privy to MK-ULTRA's existence—although the American public was never informed about the experiments—was that it was a "necessary evil" in the race against the Soviet Union to create the perfect spy.

Dissociative identity disorder (DID), once known as multiple personality disorder (MPD), was the result for many of us children, as severe trauma was used to better understand the effects of torture on mankind. Many MK-ULTRA survivors, such as myself, have continued coming forward over the decades since the 1975 Church Committee (United States Senate Select

Committee to Study Governmental Operations with Respect to Intelligence Activities) tried to expose its existence and failed.

We survivors tried again in 1995, when there was a presidential Advisory Committee on Human Radiation Experiments. Victims gave startling testimony, but thanks to the "embedded" corporate media, most of America did not hear a word about it.

Whether or not what my siblings, friends, and I went through in Omaha was part of a government conspiracy, I can't say for certain. Considering the missing children in the area at the time, not to mention the hundreds of reports of child abuse with no real investigations, it is logical to assume that the criminal drama around children was well funded and definitely well connected.

Missing, murdered, and abused children added up to a "satanic panic," in Omaha — and to this day none of the cases associated with that time has been solved or prosecuted in any way. One after another, satanic panics like the 1983 McMartin day care case in Manhattan Beach, California, in which hundreds of parents claimed that their children had been made victims of satanic practices, have fallen through the cracks. An interesting fact is that McMartin was but one of a half dozen preschools in the area accused of abuse of a similar nature (one of which was a Long Beach Catholic church), but that was kept quiet in the media.

A similar scandal occurred at the Presidio military base (which finally closed in 1995), with familiar issues that were strenuously covered up by organizations such as the False Memory Syndrome Foundation (FMSF). Years later, it was revealed that members of the early FMSF board were connected with and funded by the North American Man/Boy Love Association (NAMBLA).

The fact that the main purpose of the False Memory Syndrome Foundation has been to discredit accusations of abuse that are ritualistic, as well as satanic in nature, makes it suspect, in my opinion, as I am left to wonder why so much time and money has been invested in discrediting satanic ritual abuse and ritual abuse in general since they have already been deemed cons piracy theories in their eyes. Why waste the time and money to battle such an idea so ferociously unless there was a reason why it was necessary?

Even more currently, it is my contention that there are reasons why the Memphis Three in Arkansas, received the deal that they did, first and foremost being an attempt to prevent anyone from reconsidering the social hysteria that our nation experienced in the 1980s. It is funny, we have come to associate satanic practice with Goth kids, and yet, now, the very three we generally think of as an example have been let free because of DNA evidence. If these three aren't responsible for the satanic panic this nation experienced, then who is?

It has been my personal experience that there was more involved than just a bunch of therapists and parents trying to take down their day cares, which also explains the lockdown this nation has been under investigating such allegations.

For a long time, I just figured that my parents' friends were a bunch of sick rich pedophiles enamored of the 1960s and 1970s cinema genre of witchcraft and the Devil, like the popular Vincent Price movies portrayed at the time. Often referred to as "happenings," during these events, drunk, drugged-out narcissists paid my parents to do what they wanted with my siblings and me. (All three of my siblings are much older than I.) For many years into my young adulthood, I thought that the satanic stuff was basically their one step beyond hedonism. Bored, rich, and demented beyond reason, they assumed that my father in his high priest red robes (signifying blood sacrifice) would be their fall guy if the group were exposed. Both of my parents participated in orgies involving children, which was instrumental to Omaha's "happenings."

Satanism, however, is far more than a movie set and a red robe. Practicing the black arts leads to what lives within the shadows, and you never know what you are going to attract by dabbling in such things. Often times, those who argue that black magic doesn't work haven't personally practiced it. Having experienced it directly, I am one who believes that some doors are meant to remain shut, but fools rush in where angels fear to tread, and if anything could be said of my father it was that he was a fool.

SATANISM

"Exactly what is Satanism? Like other concepts associated with obscurity or secrecy, it is difficult to define in a precise, scientific manner. Satanism may represent an organized belief system or religion such as the Church of Satan. It may be seen merely as a vague and dramatized concept of extreme rebellion against Western norms and conventions such as the so-called 'Satanism' flaunted by some rock musicians. It may be a mythological vestige of medieval religious thinking that still lingers in modern times. It may also be a deviant practice used to intimidate and control others through ritual abuse." James Randall Noblitt and Pamela Sue Perskin, *Cult and Ritual Abuse: Its History, Anthropology, and Recent Discovery in Contemporary America* (revised edition), Westport, Conn.: Praeger, 2000 (chapter 13, Satanism? p. 153).

Both my parents were beyond imagination. My father was a violent man, abusive in every way. In his younger years he was a gangster-wanna-be, gambling, drinking, and having sex with children—his own and others. My mother was a narcissist who was aggressive and victimizing when she was inebriated. Both were intelligent and physically attractive and neither had a problem with what was occurring in our family, as both financially benefited from selling their children for sex, which there was a strong market for.

My siblings and I always believed that a demon lived inside my father as a result of his practices with the dark arts. When enraged, he became *someone else,* his gray eyes going cold like a dead fish, at which point his atrocities knew no bounds. Whoever or whatever it was, it wasn't him. Children are intuitive, and considering my parents' "social activities," it wasn't difficult to come to the conclusion that he was evil.

My father was very proud of being a generational satanist in a bloodline coven of witches. Through their associations with a group called the Colonial Dames, our family discovered we were one of the first in power within our nation beginning with the original thirteen colonies, first to arrive in America, as well as also distantly related to Beethoven, along with our satanic history. I was expected to take my place as my father's son, so my grooming began the day I was born, 12-06-66.

1

BORN TO BE THE ANTICHRIST

From conception on, I have always been considered by my father and <u>his family to be</u> the "<u>bad seed</u>." The night I was conceived, my mother had been three months or so out of the hospital after a terrible car accident in which she had both of her kneecaps ripped off, several bones broken, and suffered a serious head injury.

That night she and my father got into an argument. None of my three siblings—the youngest of whom was born twelve years before me—remembers what the argument was about, but they did remember that it became violent, and <u>my father ended up raping our mom in front of th</u>em.

When she discovered she was pregnant, my father told the family and neighborhood that he couldn't be the father because of a supposed vasectomy, although later, with another wife, he would purportedly conceive two more children. So my mother was ostracized from family, friends, and neighborhood, and I began life as the <u>bastard child</u>.

Early in the pregnancy, the family doctor had told my mother I was a tubular pregnancy and that she should abort me before I broke through (the fallopian tube) and both of us bled to death. Despite the pain she was in, she refused. Her excuse was that she was too busy, but later in life she told me she was hoping to die in order to get away from my father.

Then, one morning, she awoke and the pain was gone. If that doctor's diagnosis was correct, then I was one of the very few "ectopic" babies that found its way into the womb.

Mom went into labor on Thanksgiving night although I wasn't born until December 6, and to say I was a complicated birth is an understatement. I was breach with my hands behind my head and the resulting pressure on my mother caused her to have a stroke, flat lining her for a time. Regardless, my mother thought I was a miracle baby, which was a theme that followed me throughout childhood and adolescence.

On the other hand, my father and his friends began to impress upon me from the day I was born that I was a bad seed, supernaturally ordained to be the Antichrist.

Thus you can see how the story of my birth deeply affected my self-image. It was kind of like *The Omen,* just without the special powers. As far back as I can remember, I've feared waking up and being if not *the* Antichrist, then *an* Antichrist. Understand that I never *wanted* to be the Antichrist, but I feared that the *thing* living in my father would someday live in me and that I would somehow become like him. Assured that it was an honor, my parent's friends prepared me to embrace my fate from the very beginning, despite my horror.

Antichrist is defined in *Merriam-Webster* as one who denies or opposes Christ; *specifically:* a great antagonist expected to fill the world with wickedness but to be conquered forever by Christ at his second coming. A detailed explanation of the satanists' view of the end of days with the appearance of the Antichrist appears in the Notes at the end of this book.

It was because of this fear that I have always had an unusual relationship with God. As a child, I read everything I could about God and the Devil to find some way out of what I considered my destiny. I read the Bible again and again, studying Eastern religions, Greek mythology, and any occult book I could lay my hands on. Believing myself to be in hell and desperate to get out, I tried to kill myself several times.

As a result of my traumatic childhood, I was diagnosed with severe post-traumatic stress disorder (PTSD) and have been receiving financial assistance for over a decade from the federal SSI program. What my siblings and I went through as children "rented out" to a bunch of pedophile satanists was unspeakable enough, but add to that the devastating psychological abuse in our own family; it simply destroyed all of us.

My oldest sister and brother are dead now, one from mysterious circumstances and one from a lifetime of alcoholism and intravenous drug use. My surviving sister, whom I shall call Sarah in this book, suffers from an illness that is deteriorating her bones. And I have been in therapy for over a decade now and have actually have had to be hospitalized twice as an adult with PTSD and severe depression.

Also, I am gay. My oldest sister was always convinced it was due to the abuse I suffered as a child and that I would outgrow it, but I never have and have often come to think that being gay was my saving grace. My father and his family harped on it, further contributing to my belief that I was inherently bad. Much like the Catholic Church, my father believed it was okay to hurt children but a sin to be gay, as did his third wife—my stepmother— a narcissistic, vicious, unattractive, shrew-like Jesus freak Nazi. Twenty years his junior (a year and a half older than my oldest sister), she became my father's secretary shortly after I was born while my mother, after eighteen years of marriage, was finally divorcing him on grounds of emotional and physical cruelty.

Long before the divorce was final, my father moved in with the new lady and eventually, because his parents demanded it, married her. While my parents were complete opposites in many ways, my father and stepmother were a perfect pair (commonly referred to as a marriage made in hell, as we kids used to say). It wasn't until after my father died and I started looking into what they both were involved with that I fully began to appreciate the truth of this statement.

I stayed with my mother until I was three, at which point she abandoned my older sister (who was still living at home) and me, so we went to live with our father full-time.

Completely broken during the divorce, my mother had become a drunken prostitute, often leaving for days at time. Looking back, I now know that severe head trauma also played a part in her demise, but in those days, no one understood, so no help was available. Therefore, we were forced to live with my father and his wife.

Cinderella's stepmother was an angel compared to this woman. Unlike my mother, who had grown up elegant in her day, our father's new wife had grown up as the fat, ugly, and abused daughter of two alcoholic parents on the wrong side of the tracks. It has been my experience that she is a complete and utter sociopath. A cunning plod horse, verbally abusive and physically aggressive, she uses her belief in Jesus to justify any nasty thing she can think of, and was (and, I presume still is) a thoroughly cruel and miserable person, now a widow.

Two peas in a pod, my father and stepmother often compelled each other to new levels of bad behavior, the least of which was physical abuse. As a result, Sarah was removed from their home and placed in foster care early on, leaving me alone with two sociopaths.

But before my escape just three days after graduating from high school, I suffered through amazing abuse. The Satanism and the sexual abuse stopped when I was ten, but soon after my father and his wife became a couple of weird Christian zealots who justified abusing me for my sexual orientation, which was impossible for me to hide even at a young age. Calling me an "animal that only went off of instinct," and preaching that I "deserved to die or go to jail," and that Jesus "hated homosexuals so I would burn," I grew to associate Jesus with my abuse, believing that the beatings and assaults were because of something wrong with me and that Jesus couldn't love me.

So for years, I felt more anger than love toward Jesus, and, besides, believing you are someday going to be the Antichrist puts a damper on the whole saved-by-the-Cross idea. God was a whole other matter totally. I have always had a relationship with God, albeit tumultuous, and though I grew up often feeling abandoned by God, I never lost faith in God's existence.

Finally, in my late twenties and after getting into therapy, I discovered a spiritual practice called (Shamanism.) Usually

Shamanism

associated with the Native American medicine faith, my particular practice, as I will describe later, is more Celtic in nature. Shamanic practice involves ritual and drums that produce an effect of a "waking dream," which enables a person to symbolically explore the spiritual world that dwells within us all. Out-of-body experiences and angelic spirit guides fit well with my background of growing up believing in demons and witchcraft, though little did I know that Shamanism would eventually save my soul.

2

Alan Baer
Peter Citron } Rich Satanists
Larry King

COLD CASE FILES

Unbeknownst to the public until now, a group of rich satanists were in control of Omaha in the 1970s and 1980s. Their names are familiar: Alan Baer, Larry King, and Peter Citron, to name a few, although there are many more.

Many of the abducted or abused children who were reported (and there were plenty), as well as those who never were (which I assure you there were more of), who were not used in ritual sacrifices were being sold into a human trafficking ring. The children's names are also familiar: Ricky Chadek, Jacob Wetterling, and Johnny Gosch, for starters. Midwest law enforcement still has cold case files on them.

The public was aware that children were disappearing, but no one really knew what the disappearances meant. Parents drove kids to school and kept them indoors or at least within sight. It was a scary time in Omaha. However, even the most fantastic tales barely approach the truth, for who would believe it? I know what happened. I was forced to be part of these sick rituals.

As my father's son, I was expected to practice blood sacrifice. There is a misconception that satanists only kill babies, but it was my experience that a baby doesn't offer enough blood. In blood sacrifice, it's all about the blood, and I was taught by my father and his friends that the endorphins released into the blood when a person is under a great deal of fear and pain act as an aphrodisiac for torturers who drink the blood at the crescendo of suffering. Only elite members are allowed at sacrifices, and everyone attending was required to partake. Blood from the victim's wounds drained down an altar-like table into a chalice, from which everyone drank.

Because God forbids the spilling of blood, and satanists go against God's teachings, they exert extreme effort to spill as much blood of children as they can. High ceremonies always meant murdering young boys.

The belief that someday I would take my father's place as high priest in a highly organized but secret cult afforded me no advantage with regard to my own pain and trauma. However, I must say, the ritualistic rapes of us children by cult members were nothing in comparison to what else was happening. At what I always believed to be a local funeral home on the outskirts of town, my father and his friends furthered their enjoyment by playing horrible games of hide and seek. We children were told that if we were found, we would be killed.

All my life, I dreamed that I was often put in caskets inhabited by a corpse. Later in life, I realized these nightmares were real events and not something from my dream world. Sometimes children were buried alive in my dreams, which later was revealed as truth. And I distinctly remember, not even in a dream, that I was once forced to lie on the grave of a young boy to see if I could hear him scream. My sister later told me that they often dug the children out, but the psychological damage had already been done to me.

Many of the atrocities were proclaimed as being done in my honor, so naturally I was often forced to participate in them. Cannibalism (eating of the heart among other body parts), bestiality (forcing kids to have sex with dogs, for example), murder (sacrifices made with knives usually), and rape (of both little boys and girls) were common practice with my family's friends, and as a result, I suffered constant nightmares during my childhood and into my adult life of children coming from their graves to enact their justified revenge on me. It was because of these dreams that I would eventually seek counseling as an adult.

For me, during childhood, every day meant I could be next. Each minute was a fight for survival while my young mind struggled to find a way out of the hell I was living in, barely able to cope with the chaos I was experiencing, believing no one would listen to me if I told, and scared of the consequences I would face if I did.

In many ways, the experiences of my sisters and brother were worse than my own, given that my father was much worse when he was younger. When he wasn't selling them on the sex market, he was hog-tying them and driving around with them naked in the trunk of the car. As if he were engaged in some sort of competition as to how deviant the abuse could get, one time he and his friends buried my brother and sister in a fresh grave in Forest Lawn Cemetery up to their necks and left them after convincing them they were being left to die. My siblings told me about this when we were adults and comparing memories.

Rich, affluent, and powerful, my parents and their friends held beliefs that were well thought out and complex. Doctors, lawyers, law enforcement, high-ranking businessmen, and politicians—the people involved were community pillars, wealthy, well educated, well connected, and completely drunk on the power their group wielded.

Although there are satanists who proudly attest association with the dark arts (such as Ordo Templi Orientis (OTO), Temple of Olympus aka Ordo Astrum Serpentis, Temple of Britannia, and America's own version of a church of Satan, Temple of Set) most, of course, don't advertise their practices—probably from fear of association. Such was the case in Omaha.

As a child, I couldn't tell anyone what was happening because I couldn't trust who was involved and who wasn't, and what was happening was so crazy that I figured no one would believe me even if I told. People were adept at looking away, fearing they would somehow become involved in things too sordid to speak publically about.

A book entitled *Ritual Abuse in the Twenty-first Century: Psychological, Forensic, Social, and Political Considerations,* edited by Randy Noblitt and Pamela Perskin Noblitt, hit the bookstores in 2008. It is a collection of essays by experts who say that ritual abuse and satanic ritual abuse (which are not the same thing) happen not just today in America but are and have been a longstanding problem worldwide.

Though the book didn't address or even mention events in Omaha, it was nonetheless like reading part of my life story that held answers to childhood puzzles that had perplexed me all my life. In many ways, it was a life-changing book in that it gave me the validation I had previously lacked.

Still, there was no mention of demons, or anything that happened in Omaha. Whether the people involved were just a collection of rich wackos enamored of the Devil or involved in a government project to terrorize and dissociate victims, I experienced a strange and twisted intention behind what they were doing. I was taught there were reasons for the rituals and ceremonies, reasons why they believed a devil lived in my father, and reasons why they believed it would someday live in me.

Although this satanic knowledge was bestowed upon me as a great honor, it terrorized my entire adult life until it all came to a head on my fortieth birthday. After that, things became very strange indeed.

RITUAL ABUSE AND SATANIC RITUAL ABUSE

"For many, the notion that innocent people are deliberately, ritually traumatized is unthinkable, the stuff of science fiction novels or fantasy films. For others, it is an unspeakable but distinct reality, an experience that some say they have actually endured and continue to relive indirectly through nightmares and flashbacks. ... Many professed cult and ritual abuse survivors have reported that their perpetrators told them that no one will believe their stories" (Noblitt and Perskin, pp. xiii-xvi).

"Generations of men and women report victimization by ritual abuse perpetrated on them from early childhood. Inevitably, these informants also have severe dissociative experiences that interfere with their ability to engage in gainful employment and perform activities of daily living. Victims report that the rituals are designed to produce introjects or alter personality states who engage in various behaviors against the conscious will of the victim. Their narrations include examples of torture, deprivation, and deception, allegedly used to condition victims for use in pornography, prostitution, and other deviant or illegal activities.

"In a recent online survey [Rutz, Becker, Overkamp and Karriker, *Exploring Commonalities Reported by Adult Survivors of Extreme Abuse: Preliminary Empirical Findings,* chapter 3 in Noblitt and Noblitt, 2008], survivors of extreme abuse were invited to respond to a number of items designed to delineate the range of abuses, characteristics of the abuse, psychological and physical sequaelae, and impact on education, employment, revictimization, and interpersonal relationships. Almost 1,500 individuals from 30 different countries responded to the invitation to participate. These respondents identified their abuse experiences as including (1) incest; (2) child pornography and prostitution; (3) sexual abuse by multiple perpetrators; (4) being caged; (5) starvation; (6) bestiality; (7) buried alive; (8) electroshock; (9) sensory deprivation; (10) sleep deprivation; (11) forced cannibalism; (12) secret government-sponsored mind control experiments. Of those respondents who reported suffering extreme abuse in childhood, 55% reported abuse in a Satanic cult" (Noblitt and Noblitt, 2008, pp. 18–19).

3

SATAN WORSHIP IN AMERICA

ll satanists are *not* alike. What I am explaining speaks only for me and my experience, for there are as many divisions to Satanism as there are denominations in Christianity. Satanists have varying opinions when it comes to worship and the reasons for their practices.

Back in the 1960s, Anton Szandor LaVey (1930-1997), author of *The Satanic Bible* and a notorious cult figure, started the social experiment known as the Church of Satan. LaVey developed his church as a way to mock Christianity and the Bible: he regarded Christian theology as a collection of myths and sought to promote the other side of the argument by casting Satan as a champion for personal freedom and individuality. Reflecting the hedonism of the 1960s, the Church of Satan was an example of free love and devotion to the narcissism that was a part of the time.

Then in 1975, one of LaVey's ex-students, U.S. Army Lt. Col. Michael Aquino, broke away from the Church of Satan to found Temple of Set in San Francisco. A Satanic mimic of Martin Luther's Protestant Revolt, Aquino created a separate sect. Whereas the Church of Satan didn't believe in God and was formed basically to mock the very concept of the Christian God and Bible, Aquino's Temple of Set believed in an Antichrist who would rise and lead his followers to absolute power.

MICHAEL A. AQUINO

Michael A. Aquino, U.S. Army officer and founder of Temple of Set, is a graduate of the University of California, Santa Barbara (BA, 1968; PhD, 1980), according to answers.com and other unsubstantiated websites including YouTube and Wikipedia. In 1968 he joined the Army as a specialist in psychological warfare. The next year he joined the Church of Satan. He was ordained as a satanic priest in 1971.

Aquino rose to a position of prominence in the Church of Satan, but became dissatisfied with the leadership of church founder Anton LaVey. He opposed LaVey's arbitrary leadership and atheistic approach to religion. LaVey actually denied the existence of Satan. In 1975 Aquino sought a new mandate to operate by invoking the Devil. Satan responded by appearing as Set, the ancient Egyptian deity, and gave Aquino a document, *The Book of Coming Forth by Night*. He authorized Aquino to found the Temple of Set to supersede the Church of Satan. Aquino created a new religious society built around the worship of Set, of whom Satan is one derivation.

During the 1980s Aquino gained some degree of fame when the media became aware that an army officer led a satanic group. The temple became the subject of criticism, and Aquino was charged with tales of satanic child abuse.

Noblitt and Perskin report the following about Aquino (p. 154): "A former member of the Church of Satan, Lieutenant Colonel Michael Aquino, established his own cultic brotherhood, the Temple of Set. Although this organization also professes to be law-abiding, author Linda Blood (1994 [in *The New Satanists*, New York: Warner Books]) states that Michael Aquino was under investigation in response to child abuse allegations associated with the Presidio, an army post in California. [Blood reports] By December 1988, *San Jose Mercury News* staff writer Linda Goldston was able to report that ... [Army] authorities 'feel there is sufficient evidence to believe that a crime has been committed. The closest thing in civilian terms would be a grand jury indictment' (Blood, 1994, p. 180)."

Aquino's followers profess faith in the Egyptian God Set, brother of Isis and Osiris, as well as their arch-nemesis. Like all mystery religions, they have their own astrology, numerology, dark magic, and prophecy. In 2008, Temple of Set hosted a worldwide conference in San Francisco that members from four continents attended. Obviously, the Antichrist business is doing well.

MK-ULTRA

Now that the Catholic Church is mired in scandal for conspiring to move and hide pedophile priests for generations, people are beginning to realize that conspiracies actually do exist. The fact is, they always have. The rich and powerful have always done what they wanted, and as it is said, *power corrupts, and absolute power corrupts absolutely.*

Such was the case with MK-ULTRA and Project Artichoke, run by the CIA.

Many in Omaha at the time of my childhood believed that the Satanism being practiced in the city was linked to the government and to the local Offutt Air Force Base. Victims associated with the Franklin Credit Union (which is expanded on later) told stories of government involvement in abuse and trafficking and directly named MK-ULTRA as part of their "training."

MK-ULTRA

From Project MKULTRA, the CIA's Program of Research in Behavioral Modification (www.druglibrary.org/schaffer/history/e1950/mkultra/Hearing01.htm and *The Project MKULTRA Compendium: The CIA's Program of Research in Behavioral Modication* by Stephen Foster), which opened with Senator Edward Kennedy's remarks to a Senate investigative committee, August 3, 1977: "Some two years ago, the Senate Health Subcommittee heard chilling testimony about the human experimentation activities of the Central Intelligence Agency. The Deputy Director of the CIA revealed that over 30 universities and institutions were involved in an 'extensive testing and experimentation' program which included covert drug tests on unwitting citizens ... The best safeguard against abuses in the future is a complete public accounting of the abuses of the past."

Prepared Statement of Admiral Stansfield Turner, Director of Central Intelligence

Mr. Chairman: In my letter to you of July 15, 1977, I reported our recent discovery of seven boxes of documents related to Project MKULTRA, a closely held CIA project conducted from 1953–1964. As you may recall, MKULTRA was an "umbrella project" under which certain sensitive subprojects were funded, involving among other things research on drugs and behavioral modification. During the Rockefeller Commission and Church Committee investigations in 1975, the cryptonym became publicly known when details of the drug-related death of Dr. Frank Olsen were publicized. In 1953 Dr. Olsen, a civilian employee of the Army at Fort Detrick, leaped to his death from a hotel room window in New York City about a week after having unwittingly consumed LSD administered to him as an experiment at a meeting of LSD researchers called by CIA.

Most of what was known about the Agency's involvement with behavioral drugs during the investigations in 1975 was contained in a report on Project MKULTRA prepared by the

Inspector General's office in 1963. As a result of that report's recommendations, unwitting testing of drugs on U.S. citizens was subsequently discontinued. The MKULTRA-related report was made available to the Church Committee investigators and to the staff of Senator Kennedy's Subcommittee on Health. Until the recent discovery, it was believed that all of the MKULTRA files dealing with behavioral modification had been destroyed in 1973 on the orders of the then retiring Chief of the Office of Technical Service, with the authorization of the DCI, as has been previously reported. Almost all of the people who had had any connection with the aspects of the project which interested Senate investigators in 1975 were no longer with the Agency at that time. Thus, there was little detailed knowledge of the MKULTRA subprojects available to CIA during the Church Committee investigations. This lack of available details, moreover, was probably not wholly attributable to the destruction of MKULTRA files in 1973; the 1963 report on MKULTRA by the Inspector General notes on page 14: "Present practice is to maintain no records of the planning and approval of test programs."

Years later, when I was trying to make sense of what happened to me as a child, I began researching MK-ULTRA to see if there was any connection to my experiences. What I found was shocking.

The MK-ULTRA project seems to have originated from Germany, and the Nazi party. Its most famous member, Adolf Hitler, had an obsession with the paranormal and the occult, so during World War II, in concentration camps, horrible experiments were conducted on prisoners in an attempt to understand, amplify, and control psychic abilities that could help Germany win the war. Hitler employed hundreds of Germany's best minds, bringing them together to effectively commit atrocities against their fellow men to better understand *and control* the mind.

After Germany was defeated, the United States was determined not to allow the data from these experiments to fall into Russian hands. In 1946, President Harry Truman authorized Project Paperclip, a secret operation to bring Nazi scientists to America in hopes that they could work on our behalf during the Cold War. By 1955, more than 760 German scientists, many former Nazis, had been granted U.S. citizenship and were given prominent positions in American science as they continued their work with human psychology and the mind, among other things.

PROJECT PAPERCLIP

Rocket scientist Werner von Braun was just one of hundreds of talented scientists the U.S. brought to this country after the fall of Germany for the sole purpose of getting their advanced technology before the Russians seized the same great minds. The book *The Paperclip Conspiracy: The Hunt for the Nazi Scientists* by Tom Bower (Little, Brown, 1987) documents the rush to smuggle the scientists into the U.S. As a *New York Times* book review states (Feb. 9, 1988):

"The foremost American prizes in this grisly lottery were the leaders of German rocket research, who had either connived at or in some cases been directly involved in the use of slave labor under unspeakable conditions (in the underground rocket installations at Nordhausen, the death rate among prisoners was around 100 a day). Werner von Braun and his associates began arriving in the United States in September 1945: there were no real checks into their records or their possible complicity in major crimes."

Note that in 1951 a project called Bluebird (later renamed Artichoke) was established by the CIA, to invent techniques for special interrogations (similar to what is now being done at Guantanamo and Abu Ghraib). By using physiological and pharmacological research, the military would better understand the action or effectiveness of various agents in connection with efforts to control human behavior. In other words, mind control like the techniques portrayed in *The Men Who Stare at Goats,* is not so far fetched.

As a result of Nazi data gathered in concentration camps and delivered to the CIA, a hydra of projects were spawned, including the umbrella project MK-ULTRA, brainchild of Richard Helms, later a CIA Director, and Allen Dulles, who was CIA's Director at the time. A secret government program purportedly designed to defeat Russia in brainwashing, MK-ULTRA employed drug therapy, electroshock, sleep deprivation, memory erasure, and sensory modification, among others. These techniques are now called *enhanced interrogation,* but quite plainly they are *torture.* Unwitting victims were also exposed to radiation, lethal biological agents, and other horrors—all in the name of "national security."

In 1973, Helms, then Director of Central Intelligence, was alerted about a forthcoming congressional investigation. He therefore ordered all MK-ULTRA records to be destroyed and spread the "official" story that the program had been terminated in the late 1960s. Fortunately, 20,000 pages got overlooked. These were subsequently declassified and released (though with many redactions).

Revealing outrageous crimes against humanity perpetrated by the American government (and its contractors) on unwitting American and Canadian citizens, MK-ULTRA then surfaced for brief public attention. Most people heard about the 1975 hearings conducted by the US Senate Select Committee on Intelligence, as the mainstream media gave it page-one coverage. The hearings were chaired by Senator Frank Church (D-Idaho).

With most of the documentation destroyed and no one connected with the MK-ULTRA project working at the CIA any longer, public indignation fizzled out. Given that my experiences didn't end until 1976, and that the victims of the Franklin scandal were speaking of MK-ULTRA abuses well into the 1980s, if any of the events in Omaha are related to a "secret" government project like MK-ULTRA, then it seems that business as usual continued after the Church Committee much as before: in secret.

Books like *The Manchurian Candidate* by Richard Condon (1959) and *The Project MKULTRA Compendium: The CIA's Program of Research in Behavioral Modification* by Stephen Foster (2009) allowed me to see similarities between the objectives of the MK-ULTRA project and what was happening satanically to us as children.

Unimaginable abuse and being drugged during rituals was common, and, though the drugs probably made anal penetration less painful, they also made it difficult to determine what was real and what was not, making it easier for me to tell myself I was dreaming. A psychological attempt to shield me from the horrors I was experiencing? Perhaps. Besides ambiguity, I have to say that the drugs also added fear and terror.

Sleep deprivation came with the territory of growing up in my house, given how violent the household was. Often, my enraged father would wake us up at night and beat us; then, having worked himself into frenzy, he would rape us. As a result, I had difficulty with sleep for years into adulthood.

Although I was never diagnosed as such, my sister Sarah was diagnosed with dissociative identity disorder (DID). From what I understand about MK-ULTRA, DID was not an "offshoot" of the program, it was the goal.

DISSOCIATIVE IDENTITY DISORDER

Dissociative identity disorder (or DID) used to be known as multiple personality disorder. Most are familiar with the story of *Sybil,* a nonfiction best-seller in 1973 about a woman thought to have sixteen different personalities. The TV movie starred Sally Field and Joanne Woodward. Both book and movie brought multiple personality disorders to the forefront.

In 2011 journalist Debbie Nathan wrote *Sybil Exposed* in which she "proves" that Sybil's story was largely fabricated by a willing patient, an ambitious psychotherapist, and an imaginative journalist. Agenda driven, this book demonstrates a bait-and-switch technique that associates DID, Sybil, and our nation's history with satanic abuse together and offers a never-ending argument that distracts from the real issues of our nation's history.

The psychological community recognizes multiple personality disorder (now called DID) as an identity disorder in which two or more separate and distinct personality states (or identities) control a person's behavior at different times, according to information from the National Alliance on Mental Illness (NAMI).

When under the control of one identity, the person is usually unable to remember some of the events that occurred while other personalities were in control. The different identities, referred to as *alters,* may exhibit differences in speech, mannerisms, attitudes, thoughts, and gender orientation. The alters may even differ in "physical" properties such as allergies, right-or-left handedness, or the need for eyeglass prescriptions. These differences between alters are often quite striking.

At the time that a person with DID first seeks professional help, he or she is usually not aware of the condition. A very common complaint in people with DID is episodes of amnesia, or time loss.

These individuals may be unable to remember events in all or part of a time period.

Retrieving and dealing with memories of trauma is important for the person with DID, because *this disorder is believed to be caused by physical or sexual abuse in childhood.* Young children have a pronounced ability to dissociate (much like daydreaming is a form of dissociation), and it is believed that those who are abused may learn to use dissociation as a defense. In effect, the child slips into a state of mind in which it seems that the abuse is not really occurring to him or her, but to somebody else. In time, such a child may begin to split off alter identities. Research has shown that the average age for the initial development of alters is 5.9 years.

Children with DID have a great variety of symptoms, including depressive tendencies, anxiety, conduct problems, episodes of amnesia, difficulty paying attention in school, and hallucinations. Often these children are misdiagnosed as having schizophrenia. By the time the child reaches adolescence, it is easier for a mental health professional to recognize the symptoms and make a diagnosis of DID.

Breaking the mind into compartments and afterward programming the different compartments for different functions was part of building spies and assassins. Our experiences might also have been designed to effectively cause psychotic breaks. Whatever the objectives at the time, in the end it basically destroyed our psyches. Most of the torture could have been some sort of bizarre experiment, but certain events make me wonder if what we went through wasn't intentional *programming.*

The following memory was never a dream. I just knew this happened. When I was about seven, I was brought into a room in which a dark-haired boy sat with a dog and three men. Judging from how the boy was clinging to the animal, I believed it to be his dog, but looking back I realize he could have been clinging to the dog out of fear.

While being intensely observed, I was forced to watch as the boy was first tortured with cigarette burns and threats of death, then forced to kill his dog with a knife. Afterward, sobbing and terrified, he was tied to the chair. I was told he was weak and therefore unworthy to live. As a tribute to me, I was ordered to kill him and release him from his life bonds.

Saying "no" under such circumstances, especially as a child, was not an option, but even so I found myself unable to commit such an act. I complained that I couldn't do it because he was looking at me, my hope being that my excuse would excuse me from committing murder.

The men were not to be daunted. Grabbing hold of the boy's head, proclaiming they were doing it in my honor, they removed his eyes with a scalpel. I still hear the boy's screams. Once they realized that the screams were bothering me, they removed his tongue. The sounds of his gurgling screams were finally enough; I plunged the knife handed to me into his chest.

The point of this ritual I can't say, but I remember that the men didn't take their eyes off me. Whether it was a government project or a ritual committed by fanatical weirdoes, try as I may, I will never forget those eyes.

Psychic ability was expected, and I was taught at an early age how to look into a person's eyes to figure out what they were afraid of. I was also taught that there are three kinds of people: the material, basic cattle to be used at will, sometimes referred to as "eaters and breeders"; the psychic, who can be ambassadors to the third type; which is the spiritual, the level I was expected to achieve.

Because I was encouraged to open myself up and trust my intuition early, this may have been why my father, who eventually came to fear me, told me on a daily basis that I was "an animal who only went on instinct." Having an idea of things I was being trained for, I imagine I made him uncomfortable, and for many years I hated my father. In fact, like a good satanist, I hated both my parents.

[Note: when I say "my parents," I generally mean my father and stepmother if I am referring to my life up to age eighteen. After that I lived again with my mother. My father was married three times. His first wife does not figure in this book. His second wife, my mother, had five offspring—me being her youngest. His third wife is the one I call stepmother.]

DARK CELEBRATIONS *Michael Aquino*

With risk of jumping too far ahead of myself, I need to make a further introduction in order to help put what I have explained into perspective. As a child in all of this, you need to understand that no introductions were ever made, and no explanations were ever offered. Having the perceptions of a child, I focused on what I needed to survive, and little else. What I was being forced to do took more of a precedent than who was making me do it, and the question of why didn't factor into things until long into my adulthood.

Sedation beforehand and electro shocks to my head afterward helped me forget a lot of it, keeping my experiences in a fog that only manifested in my dreams. Never wanting to look back and remember, I was adept at avoiding the past until, although it wouldn't happen until well into my adulthood, I would see the man in my dreams, which changed everything for me.

My worst nightmares both as a child and as an adult always involved a man I believed to be a figment of my imagination. Always elaborately dressed in long and flowing attire, he was a gay version of Eddie Munster from the popular television show in the '70s, as flamboyant as he was sadistic, and evil to the core. He dominated my dreams, and often my waking life, but it wasn't until after my father's death in 2006 when I began to research my past that I discovered that the man of my dreams was an actual living breathing person. It was this realization that began to put everything into perspective for me.

It is hard to explain what it was like to see Col. Michael Aquino for the first time as an adult. Just seeing a video of the man being interviewed on a national talk show physically sucked the air from my lungs, leaving me unable to breathe for a while.

As you will read, for many years I did everything I could to disassociate myself from my childhood, trying to escape the effects of my past any way possible. But all that changed when I laid eyes on the man who had tormented my memories and dreams all my life, thus making it impossible to deny my past any longer.

I guess the first thing you need to understand about Michael Aquino is that people are afraid of him, not because he is a founder of the satanic cult Temple of Set, but rather the people he is associated with are those who scare others. He likes to hang with nasty people, who like to do nasty things, and they are all connected to the government and projects that no one really likes to talk about.

Good friends with both presidents Reagan and Bush, Sr., he has a long distinguished career in psych ops and, among other things, was a person accused of satanically abusing children at the Presidio day care. He was also my main handler in the instruction and practice of black magic. It takes a man of strong convictions to build a temple to practice his faith, and Temple of Set stands as a testimony to Aquino's fortitude to further explore concepts most would rather deny existed, as does his distinguished military career.

Had he not shared his exuberance for celebrating the dark with me as a child, I would not understand what I do today, looking back. As much as he would hate to admit it, I am a testament to his brilliance.

GROWING UP IN PARADISE

Being groomed to be a psychopath lasted until I was ten, at which time the father of an abducted girl caused my family's circumstances to take a turn for the worse (though in the end this would save my life).

In the 1970s in Omaha an inordinate number of child abductions were occurring, including murders. During that time, a dark-haired little girl, a playmate of mine, who lived a few blocks from us disappeared.

Soon afterward, my parents and I moved out of Omaha to a small town forty-five minutes away. I didn't think much about the move until the summer of 1976, when the deceased girl's father knocked on our door. Still desperate to find his little girl and knowing that she and I had been playmates, he'd tracked us down years after the fact. He wanted to know if my family knew anything about her disappearance.

Inviting him in, my father sat with him in our living room as my stepmother prepared refreshments in the kitchen, drugging his iced tea. They waited until he passed out, then dragged him into the basement and tied him to a chair.

My father then called my oldest sister Cindy and my older brother Stephen, both of whom did the bidding of my father until the day he died. With my stepmother, they decided to perform a ritual of our own, without the help of my father's friends. They were all panicking and they needed to involve me to ensure my silence, so as a group they decided I could handle what they were about to make me do.

Desperate times call for desperate measures, as they say, and so late that night, as we surrounded the unconscious man tied to a chair, my father doused him with lighter fluid, and my stepmother handed me the match that I was forced to throw on the man, thus lighting him on fire.

He woke up instantly and his screams pierced the confines of our basement. I stood with my hands over my ears. Grabbing a shovel, my father plunged it into his stomach and silenced him instantly. My stepmother then ordered me to my room where I sat huddled in a corner for the rest of the night. Afterward, we quickly moved out of state to a small town in northern Iowa where I would live until age eighteen.

The damage from that night triggered my post-traumatic stress disorder, well known today among soldiers. Plagued by nightmares, I became unable to control my emotional out-bursts, posing a threat to my family, so my father and stepmother stepped up my physical abuse until I had a psychotic break at twelve.

Not knowing what to do with me, they sent me to stay the summer with my older sister Sarah in Minnesota, who was then twenty-four. She had been removed from their care in childhood and placed in foster care and had eventually moved north to escape our father.

Post-Traumatic Stress Disorder (PTSD)

Post-traumatic stress disorder (known as PTSD) is a type of anxiety disorder. It can occur after someone has seen or experienced a traumatic event that involved the threat of injury or death. Soldiers can experience PTSD after a disturbing combat experience. But so can people in a car accident or victims of domestic abuse.

PTSD changes the body's response to stress. It affects the stress hormones and chemicals that carry information between the nerves (neurotransmitters).

Some people relive the event through flashbacks or nightmares or uncomfortable situations that remind them of the event. Others feel an emotional numbing, detachment, and are unable to remember important aspects of the trauma. Others find themselves hypervigilant—startled by any loud noise. People with PTSD may have trouble falling asleep or may be irritable and show outbursts of anger, according to the National Institutes of Health.

Sarah had her hands full with me, given how I constantly lied about everything and stole from her friends. She was also involved in a physically abusive relationship with her first husband at the time, struggling to overcome her own childhood experiences. She was patient with me until the day I physically attacked her son, at which point she called the police. The details of what happened are unimportant, but immediately after attacking her child, I tried to kill myself by taking pills I found in her medicine cabinet.

For the first time, not only were the police involved but doctors and social workers as well, and they all wanted to know why I was having a psychotic break. After telling them that I was the Antichrist and needed to die, and after listening to my sister's explanation as to what she believed I was going through, the Minnesota courts ordered social workers to monitor my father's house in Iowa after I was returned to him.

The small town in Iowa where we lived was isolated (thirty minutes from the Minnesota border), and everyone saw us as a bunch of weirdoes. I was psychologically fractured and unable to hide the fact that I was gay, so I grew up with no real friends. Lonely, angry, and hopeless, a month after returning to my father's house and convinced I was saving the world, I tried to kill myself again. Thanks to a social worker, I ended up being looked after in a mental hospital for five months, which was a life-changing event.

When I'm asked how I survived what I went through as a child, I always look back on the events leading up to my hospital stay as a time when things began taking a different turn. Though unable to convince myself that I wasn't the Antichrist, it was the first time in my life that I wasn't being abused, and as a result I began to realize that abuse didn't have to be a way of life. At thirteen, this was a major revelation.

Another revelation was that I was of above-average intelligence. Having no self-esteem after being told by my father and stepmother that I was not only evil but also stupid, I learned early to distrust my perceptions concerning what was going on around me. My reality was constantly being rewritten by my parents, as they denied their actions of abuse. In other words, I was constantly being told that what I knew to be true was not true, and as a result, I came to distrust my own experiences and intelligence.

Those five months in the hospital gave me a chance to explore who I was without my father, stepmother, and their friends rewriting me. No one believed me when I told them what had been going on at home all my life; nonetheless, I felt a freedom I had never felt before.

Although the hospital recommended a group home after my stay, I reluctantly agreed to return home with my father after a tearful reunion. Other than when I was admitted—when he asked why I didn't just "jump in front of a train"—it was the only other time he was to visit me, though he sent his wife one other time to attend a family counseling session.

Still, I loved him, and though I knew the physical and emotional abuse would continue, I figured it was better to return to what I knew rather than take the chance on something new. Years later, my therapist told me this was typical of abuse survivors, but I chided myself for years afterward for my decision. However, everything happens for a reason, and this was no different. Try as they might, neither my father nor his third wife could beat out of me the budding self-confidence that began during my stay in the hospital.

Returning as a gay mental patient, whom my father belittled every chance he could, I was pretty much a leper at thirteen. At the local café, he told everyone I was a "crazy fag." In fact, discrediting me became a lifetime commitment not only for my father but for most of his family as well; then there was my own bizarre behavior.

To keep everyone at a distance, I told fantastic tales about my biological mother. Constantly uptight, I disrupted classes and spent much of my school day roaming the hallways. Unable to hide the fact that I was weird but unable to tell anyone why, I spent a lot of time trying to say and do the right things to fit in, but failed miserably.

Being gay in the early 1980s in small town Iowa was anything but well received. Yet being gay gave me my first sense of identity and made me strong in the face of continuing abuse, although it alienated me from my peers.

It was worse than being bullied; everyone went out of their way to avoid me. Having no friends other than teachers, I excelled on stage and played every lead in every play from freshman to senior year. I owe my drama teacher Ms. J more than I can ever repay as she gave me the opportunity to escape my life by giving me the chance to be someone else during my high school years, as well as giving me a safe place to go. My fellow classmates laughed at me, and with only thirty-one people in my graduating class, I spent years being the class joke.

Humiliated by the physical abuse I was enduring and having no one to tell, God became my only confidant, and believing in the training I had undergone as a child, I convinced myself that I could sense God in the elements around me. My relationship with God would be one of the few constants I could count on in my life. I suppressed my conviction that I was the Antichrist and went out of my way to make God proud of me, probably because no one else in my life liked me, hoping I would be able to skip the whole responsibility of being the Bringer of Doom and all.

In my later teens, I grew taller and beefier than my father and began to fight back. I was never brave enough to strike my father or stepmother, but I spent a great deal of time verbally fighting back, which at first made the physical abuse worse. However, a person can only be treated like an animal for so long before he has no choice but to fight back, and by my late teens I had reached the point where enough was enough.

Highly intelligent, I became good at mind games. Once, hiding a butcher knife in my bedroom, I waited days for my stepmother to find it, knowing that she routinely went through my things. Finally one day I came home to find her hysterical and convinced that I was planning to kill her and my father in their bed at night. After that, she began to think twice about beating me. It was harsh but effective, because I used their own sense of paranoia against them and slept better for it.

Three days after graduating from high school in 1985, I left their house forever. At the time I had no idea where I was going or what I would do, but any place was better than where I was.

4

RETURNING TO WONDERLAND

fter roaming around the Midwest, thumbing rides and befriending people with cars for the summer and living off the compassion of strangers, I found myself living with an older man who was kind enough to offer me a place to stay until I got on my feet. After a few months, with no job, no car, no money, no hope for a future, and constantly fearing when the other shoe would drop, I once again grew depressed and decided to kill myself. At nineteen, death had become preferable to what I was afraid would happen in my future.

I waited one morning for my friend to leave, then blew out the pilot lights on the gas stove and sat down, expecting the gas to eventually overwhelm me. Five minutes later, however, I received a call from my sister Cindy who, sensing something was wrong, asked me what I was doing.

After I told her I was waiting to die, she convinced me to turn off the gas. She called back five minutes later and told me that our mother—our real mother, not our ugly stepmother—needed help. She was just getting out of the hospital after drinking herself into a diabetic coma and was willing to wire me a bus ticket to come back to Omaha. Having no idea who my mother was as a person, and from the stories my family told me expecting the worst, I nonetheless agreed. The next day, I returned to Wonderland.

According to my family, my mother had come back from the hospital a completely different person after her car accident the year before I was born. Once driven, brilliant, outgoing, and ambitious, she had become a binge drinker and a bar fly, commonly taking men home from the bar and making a few bucks in the process. "Drunken slut," "whore," and "skank" were words often used to describe her. I remember the venom dripping whenever my father and his family would speak of her, which would generally be directed at me for being "my mother's son."

I had a great deal of rage against her for abandoning me, but my anger was nothing compared to that of my older siblings who blamed her for our entire dysfunctional childhood. Too weak to save us from our father, she was best friends with many of the pedophiles who abused us. My siblings held her responsible for my father's actions in a way that I, who was much younger, never quite understood. Years later, I realized that my oldest sister and brother probably never felt safe showing their anger toward our father, so they directed most of their blame toward our mother.

Although I too was angry with her, I still loved her, and in many ways it was hard not to feel sorry for her. Abandoned by everyone in the family, she had spent her life in and out of hospitals and now she'd drunk herself into a diabetic coma and had been repeatedly raped for two weeks by her roommate, a disgusting old troll drinking buddy. Had another friend of hers, worried, not come to check on her and called an ambulance, she would have died. This was her pattern.

Another time she fell in the snow, passed out for eight hours, and got frostbite. Before that, she'd spilled a thirty-two-cup coffee urn over herself causing third-degree burns. The list went on, always hurting herself while drunk, sometimes spending weeks at a time drunk with drinking buddies and glasses of Gordon's gin—chilled, no ice.

As with most binge drinkers, she was a Jekyll and Hyde. After moving in with her, I discovered a completely different side to her when she wasn't drinking. Gracious, intelligent, and funny, my mother wasn't the one-dimensional being my family made her out to be. Although the relationship was awkward at first, given that neither of us had any idea who the other was, we eventually grew quite close, becoming friends as well as mother and son, although her drinking would be a problem until her kidneys failed and killed her in the end.

Coming together was not an easy process. Conflicted, I bounced between hating her and needing her desperately. With little respect for her and her drinking, and constantly angry due to the abuse I had just escaped from, I wasn't much of a caregiver. I blamed her for abandoning me and resented the fact that I now had to take care of her. I would often fly into loud fits of outrage, screaming at her about the indignities of my abuse. Desperate to reach out to me, she endured my rants quietly; in the end she expressed her sorrow and regret for what had happened.

For my part, I was angry with God, the world, and myself, and I began shoplifting and experimenting with drugs, which infuriated her. I don't wish to give the impression that my mother was timid and quiet, for just the opposite was true. She was one of the most opinionated and outspoken women I have ever known and often voiced her disapproval over the choices I was making. Concerned that my anger would one day get me into trouble, she would often tell me to go "beat a tree" and "yell at the wind."

Strong-willed and spiritual, she constantly urged me to seek out God, in whom she believed emphatically, though she disliked religion. She urged me to talk with her, to use her as a sounding board so that things would stop eating me up inside. As a result, we had long dinner conversations in which, for the first time, someone was actually willing to listen to me.

But that was when she wasn't drunk and calling the police at three o'clock in the morning, having them wake me up to throw me out. Gin made my mother mean, and the care she offered me when she was sober dissipated the more she drank. The worst alcoholic I have ever seen, my mother would spend weeks sober and then would spend just as much time consuming gin.

During drunken episodes, she would sit in a chair and drink for weeks, often not getting up to eat, sleep, or urinate, surrounding herself with "friends" such as the one who raped her for two weeks, who would enable her to drink nonstop for weeks at a time. They often showed up during the first two weeks of the month when she got her disability check, always disappearing when the money ran out.

Sooner more than later, they would be the least of my worries, as the past was about to come a calling; the wind was building, bringing a storm that would wash over me. As the second witch in Shakespeare's Macbeth predicted: "Something wicked this way comes."

THE PRINCE OF TEMPTATION

BJ was in his early twenties, newly married with a wife expecting, and living in the apartment downstairs from my mother. Hearing all about me from my mother the night before I arrived, he anticipated my arrival before I even knew him. Bisexual, he was excited to have a gay man living in the same building, although it turned out I was nothing like he expected. Later commenting that I dressed like some sort of "preppy Jehovah's Witness" (and having a grandfather who was an elder in the church, he would know), we nonetheless struck up a friendship.

To me, he was a paradox: married and yet an effeminate gay man. And though I wasn't attracted to him in a sexual sense, I found him intriguing. Both he and his wife were physically stunning. However, he was physically small and suffered from a "Napoleon complex." Far from weak, one of the first stories he related was how it took eight or nine police to subdue him just a few months before when he'd gotten drunk and out of control. Prone to violent rages, he had a severe problem with alcohol, but I didn't know any of this yet.

He was the first person my own age I had ever met who knew what it was like to be gay. We struck a bond immediately. Friendly, personable, and—I would later learn—a complete mess, as we got to know each other, we realized that we both had survived terrible abuse. He'd lived the majority of his life in Omaha, and his parents were a weird opposite to mine: his father the alcoholic and his mother the sociopath aggressor. The fact that our abuse was similar in severity was what bonded us tightly for better or worse.

BJ's basement apartment was immaculately clean except for the countless cats; their fur and smell permeated everything. His beautiful wife lacked all social graces, was overbearing, and generally hard to take; of course, I didn't realize this the first night. I gladly accepted a dinner invitation from them, happy to finally have people my own age in my life, although later I would find out that the delicious steak sandwiches BJ and his wife served that night originated from my mother's freezer. Stealing my own food and graciously serving it to me was just a small indication of the darkness BJ promised, but at the time I was just glad to have a friend, not knowing that the fun was just getting ready to begin. *John Joubert*

AT THE GATES OF HADES

Omaha is a much different place today than it was in 1986. After all the child abductions and ritualistic murders, citizens were breathing a collective sigh of relief after the arrest of John Joseph Joubert. A twenty-year-old radar technician stationed at Offutt, he was caught in January the year before for killing two paperboys. Although he had absolutely no connection to previously abducted paperboys such as Johnny Gosch in Des Moines, or to the murders of previously discovered children, it was something, and citizens were beginning to feel safe.

JOHNNY GOSCH

Johnny Gosch 'Sighted Alive' with Abductors, January 29, 1984, *Omaha World-Herald:* Johnny Gosch, victim of one of the nation's most notorious child kidnappings, reportedly has been sighted alive with his abductors. His mother, Noreen, said she was notified Wednesday that the FBI and a Chicago detective agency had confirmed a report that the boy tried to escape from his captors in a Southwestern city.

Johnny was 12 when he was abducted in West Des Moines, Iowa, by two men who pulled him into a car when he was delivering newspapers the morning of Sept. 5, 1982. [Gosch has never been found dead or alive.]

Like almost everywhere in America in the 1980s, drugs were flowing, and especially in the gay community in Omaha, where it was touted one could find the best drugs. Rumors abounded about sex parties with children present, drug-enhanced orgies attended by the elite somehow connected to abducted children, but I wouldn't hear about these rumors until later on, and it would be even longer before I connected my childhood experiences to those rumors.

At nineteen and new to Omaha as a young man, the gay lifestyle seemed like paradise as I was finally able to be myself.

From my experience as a homosexual, there are three types of gay guys. First, there is the homosexual, a person who just happens to have sex with another person of the same sex. Then there are gay people, activists hanging out at the Castro in San Francisco, joining bowling clubs, attending social events, and generally hanging out with those who, if not gay, were still open-minded.

Then there is the third type. Jaded, bitter, and critical, a fag will use anyone to achieve whatever he is interested in at the moment—drugs, money, sex, position, it doesn't matter. Feeling a sense of entitlement either because he is young, desirable, powerful, or rich, he lives a life of hedonism, never once concerning himself with the pain his narcissistic lifestyle causes others. In the 1980s, power in the gay world was concentrated in this third type, and though many of them were married, they nonetheless were fucking anyone and everyone they could and causing chaos in all the lives they touched.

A month after my return, my mother received a call from another of her shady friends who wasn't interested in drinking but wanted to meet me.

"Dick called. A little bird told him you were in town," my mother related the conversation. "He wants to meet you. He might offer you a job."

"Is he cool?" I asked her. My mother's friends were either alcoholics or connected to our stuff in the past, and I was always skeptical about meeting any of her friends.

She assured me he was on the up and up. So for a prospective job opportunity, I agreed to visit with him.

Dick Bishop's name fit him, for rumor had it that although he may have been small in stature, he was endowed with a very large penis, which he paraded around like a strange circus act. A member of a wealthy Omaha family in the office cleaning business, he had become a flaming homosexual interior designer and held large parties at his 15,000-square-foot, colonial-style mansion in the historic Cathedral area on North Thirty-Eighth.

As an honorary member of the Hell's Angels, he often invited motorcycle clubs to his parties that ended in orgies in the upstairs rooms. Actually, there was more to the story, a lot more, as I found out later.

Our first meeting was uneventful. He came to my mother's apartment and stayed just long enough to size me up, asking about my education, and appearing to appreciate my manners and intelligence. He asked if I would like to come to his house at a later date to discuss a job in his interior design company, which excited me. That a wealthy business owner would show interest in me gave me a real lift, and I readily agreed.

Before leaving, however, he made a strange comment about how much better looking I was than my brother. Assuming it was pure flattery and that he was making a play for me, I blew it off. Still, it struck me as odd. Later, I asked my mother how Dick knew my older brother. Quickly, she replied that they had met once, and then changed the subject.

IN THE DEVIL'S DEN

Dick's job offer was nothing like what I was expecting. I met him at his lavish mansion a week later and was told that I would be maintaining his house—dusting and vacuuming as well as cleaning the pool daily once it got warm. He was about to leave for his vacation house in Hawaii and planned to return in a couple of months. He hired me, solidifying the deal by handing me a roll of money—$1,000. More money than I had ever seen in my young life. Assuring me that it would be wonderful, he grabbed hold of my butt as I got up to leave. Not wanting to throw a fit, I decided to ignore it, figuring I would deal with it if the time ever came.

At nineteen and having gone through what I'd gone through, I could be a pretty docile kind of guy. Sexual abuse has an effect on a person's psyche, and coming from years of isolation, I was desperate for attention. Not that I would ever have sex with Dick, money or not, but I figured that a grab now and then was no big deal. Laughing it off, I walked out with a job and a thousand dollars richer.

I was attractive, but never felt like it. In high school, I'd been plagued with terrible acne. At 6 feet 2 inches and 160 pounds, I'd jogged ten miles a day in that isolated Iowa town because running connected me with God in a way nothing else did, and it was a wonderful escape. Being the first in town to own a Walkman, I would lose myself in my runs, forgetting the suffering that I had to endure at home. I was scolded for eating too much chocolate, but the truth is I hardly ate anything, let alone chocolate, given that I had no job or money.

My father and stepmother commonly referred to me as "zit head" and "pimple face"; mysteriously, the acne cleared up a few weeks after I escaped their house. Regardless, I still felt like an ugly, stupid, useless piece of crap whenever I looked in the mirror, and I still looked too thin in my clothes.

My mother was binge drinking on and off during this time, and when she was sober, she would tell me to "look straight ahead, do my job, and get the cash." So while Dick was gone, I went to the downtown Old Market to get a job. Kids gravitated to this trendy cobblestoned warehouse district with upscale restaurants and shops because back then it was *the* place to be if you were anyone, and figuring it was as good a place as any to get a job, I procured my first job at Stars Restaurant—a dark underground bar and eatery accessed by concrete stairs from the street level.

Billed as a gay establishment, it nonetheless served a diverse crowd, though many of them were indeed gay. Unfortunately in the month and a half that I worked there, I was reintroduced to the seedy side of Omaha. I wasn't much of a waiter, but by flirting with patrons, I discovered that men were bringing in young boys they called "trade." Sensing a connection with the

Godfather's Pizza upstairs, I began to grow uncomfortable with the situation.

Having been nicknamed Prudence at a party for refusing sex, I viewed the sordid way sex was being manipulated as wrong, but needing the job, I did what everyone else seemed to do and looked away; while I rejected my own offers with a smile, I always walked away feeling disgusted and dirty.

When I told my drunken mother about what I thought was going on at Stars, she would say cryptic things like, "You don't know what you're dealing with" and that I should "get out now, while I still could." Later, when she was sober, I'd ask her what she meant, but she would always dismiss it as the drink talking and change the subject.

BJ was the only other person I told. Laughing it off, he'd say there was nothing wrong in making a buck, and if I wanted to, he could introduce me to some people. Horrified at the prospect of prostituting myself, I declined, though secretly I was intrigued that he knew such people.

Finally, unable to deal with the fact that child prostitution was taking place, my paranoia got the best of me and I quit. I figured my mother would be dismayed, but she seemed relieved. "Just get another job" was all she said.

Escaping Stars and thinking I was better for it, I had no idea that I was just beginning my journey into the Devil's den, nor did I realize that my curiosity about BJ's offer would get the better of me in the end. Unconcerned at the time, I figured there was always the job with Dick to look forward to.

THE RUN

As a young gay kid technically unable to get into the bars legally until I was twenty-one, there was very little to do other than hang out at a place in town called The Run, a two-block radius surrounding the local jail a few blocks up from the Old Market. The Greyhound bus station was across the street, and around the corner was a bar also called The Run that allowed teens in after one in the morning for dancing on weekends, making it a popular place for teenagers.

Men drove around the block over and over to pick up tricks and trade, tricks being sexual hookups and trade prostitution. Boys walked around the jail, selling themselves sometimes at twenty bucks a pop. There could be thirty to forty teenage boys or more, either hanging out on the wall by the Greyhound bus station or sitting in their cars in the parking lot, making it a veritable meat market for old trolls looking for sex.

The Run bar was something else altogether. Dark, smelly, and generally filled with falling down drunks, it was the only place for teens to go on weekends. At one o'clock, the staff would empty the bar, clean the glasses, put the alcohol away, and open a half hour later for after-hours dancing that lasted until four in the morning. As a result, The Run was packed every weekend.

I've heard that nothing good happens after one in the morning, and looking back on what was happening on The Run, I'd have to agree. As a kid, it was exciting and fun, but now I realize how dangerous The Run was. Besides prostitution, there were always fights or "fag bashing": uncomfortable straight boys with their girlfriends dancing at The Run were hit on by a gay guy in the bar, which usually brought fists flying.

Another bar called The Hollywood, across the street and half a block down from the police station, had been torn down by the city after allegations that child pornography was being filmed in the dungeon of the establishment. Once brought to the place when I was fifteen, it wasn't hard for me to believe the rumors that snuff films (porn ending in murder) were being filmed down there, but instead of investigating the allegations, the city decided to tear down the bar and put up a parking garage.

Across from the police station was a bar called The Stage Door, right up the street from The Hollywood. It was a hot spot at the time, but the manager quit after being accused by the Des Moines mother of paperboy Johnny Gosch of being involved in his 1982 abduction. Once again, there was no investigation into the allegations, nor any investigation into Gosch's disappearance whatsoever, but those who heard about the situation figured Sam Soda, the manager of The Stage Door, left just to avoid any problems. *Sam Soda*

Behind the police station was another bar called The Max, a one-room crap hole whose doorman was Tank, an unattractive middle-aged man who allowed minors into the bar if they submitted to a blow job. Finding the prospect distasteful, I declined and thus alienated myself from the bar for a time.

A couple of years or so before the whole Franklin Credit Union went sour, The Max went from being a one-room shit hole to a five-bar extravaganza in a matter of a year and a half and, with a state-of-the-art light and sound system, became the nation's most talked about gay bar. If rumors are true, it owed its overnight success to helping Franklin launder $40 million of bilked money.

So by the middle of the 1980s Omaha's gay lifestyle was pretty out of control on The Run and in the bars. *Corrupt* would be the word I'd use to describe it. Corruption has its own entertainment factor, though, and most of the participants were too busy having fun to notice what was wrong.

5

THE DENIAL
OF EXISTENCE

After what happened in my childhood, why would I return to Omaha? For the longest time, I had no answer. Even after years of therapy later in life, my reasoning was vague, claiming that I had nowhere to go other than my mother's, so I did what I had to do. It took years of therapy before I would even let myself think about what had happened in my past. I was in complete denial, as is common with abused children, and I lied more to myself than anyone else.

Since childhood, I'd done everything I could to deny my existence and pretend I was somebody different. Lying to yourself can be very effective, especially when you so desperately want to believe it. I dismissed the memories of the physical and emotional torture I had endured at the hands of my father and his friends as mere imaginings. I was accustomed to living in chaos and denying that anything was the matter, so I continued doing what I had learned to do: overlooking and dismissing what I was experiencing. Inevitably, I taught myself to avoid consciously thinking about the trauma I'd gone through.

But denial has a strange effect on the psyche, and being a liar takes its toll on the soul. By refusing to deal with what had happened to me as a child, my mind continued processing the truth in other ways: constant nightmares, the inability to sleep, fear of what I would see in dreams. Sleep deprivation heightened my already erratic sense of fight or flight, so I panicked over nothing and the stress added to the paranoia I felt, further alienating me from myself.

Later, through therapy, I discovered that I was experiencing post-traumatic stress disorder (PTSD) due to (1) the satanic ritual abuse I had suffered as a young child *and* (2) the ritual abuse I suffered under my father and stepmother. Ritual abuse is simply abuse dealt out on a daily basis to the point that being beaten and treated like an animal becomes the everyday norm. Both ritual abuse and satanic abuse impact the victim, and for a long time it was just easier to observe the ordinary abuse and keep the bizarre, scary stuff buried deep.

To survive in my father's house, I had spent most of my time in my room with my nose in a book, a psychological pattern that carried into my young adulthood. Books offered an escape fundamental to my survival for many years. They allowed me brief moments of living imaginatively in realities other than my own. Years of hours alone in my room was how I learned to live in my head where I could read, journal, and talk to God.

Often dark and cynical, I spent an inordinate amount of time worrying about when the next bad thing was going to happen. Overwhelmed at home, I fought deep self-destructive periods of depression and hopelessness. Dealing with my mother's alcoholism as a young adult was more of the same, and in the end I stopped caring so as to avoid my constant feelings of rage and depression. Under the vise grip of severe stress, not caring became my only way to cope. Deny, lie, and look the other way became my motto.

Grasping at straws of a severely challenged self-identity, I spent a lot of time focusing on the fact that I was gay. I had used it as a weapon in order to embarrass my father and his wife in our small town, and they had used it to beat me down. Their horror at having someone call and ask if the faggot was home gave me a certain satisfaction, the only trophy I could come away with. It always hurt me deep down though, because I believed that being gay was just one more indication of my future as the Antichrist.

Quite honestly, as a child I would have given anything not to be gay. I was conflicted, battling what I believed to be right, such as the fundamentalist conviction that homosexuality was wrong, in comparison to whom I was. Growing up, I learned to treat my sexuality as a sword and shield, striking at my father and stepmother's hypocritical sense of propriety, while at the same time shielding myself, using it as a way to distance myself from others so I could feel safe.

Safety and the inability to feel safe have been strong constants in my life. Growing up I did have the stability of a roof over my head and clothes on my back, but rarely ever did I feel safe. Beatings and living with people who consider you an animal is never a safe or healthy environment, and outings with my father and his family always ended in arguments as I would often become enraged by their comments about my sexuality and fire back my own insults. I was also never allowed to forget that I was my mother's son.

My mother accepted my sexuality without question, remarking when I told her about being gay, "Thank God, now one of my children will have some taste." It was because of this that I first grew to trust, then to love my mom. She may have been the worst, the dirtiest, the most promiscuous alcoholic I have ever known, but she loved me, and for a long time in my life she was all I had.

THE PRINCE OF CHARMS

Have you ever met someone for the first time and felt as if you have known them forever, like you'd been friends in another life?

I have only felt this way a few times in my life, and David Klotz was the first. He was standing outside The Run in jeans and a black fringe jacket that was all the rage of the 1980s, while I was waiting with my friend Mark Anderson for after-hours to open.

Mark was a really cool older guy who had befriended me a few weeks after I arrived in Omaha. He showed me Omaha on his motorcycle and never made a pass at me. I felt comfortable with him, and for a while I fell under his protective wing. Mark introduced me to David and we began to talk, our conversation lasting all night. We were never sexual, but I instantly felt brotherhood between David and me. After dancing, I invited David back to my mom's so we could keep talking until early morning about God, creation, the universe, and life as we knew it.

Other than BJ, it was the first time I'd spoken with someone my age about the things that interested me, and David was no slouch when it came to his own philosophy on life. A year younger than I, he had also come from a chaotic background, which was probably why he veered toward danger his whole life.

An only child in an upper-middle-class family, his father had been career military, and his mother was a social climber homemaker. Both of David's parents were disinterested in him, and they pretty much abandoned him as soon as they could legally do so. He'd gone into the armed services to get an education, but after stealing a bunkmate's boom box and almost being strangled to death, he got thrown out with a dishonorable discharge. That was fine by David, just as long as he got out.

Although he was incredibly personable and funny, growing up gay as an only child in a disapproving household was lonely for David. Whereas I blamed God and raged over the injustices in my life, David believed that everything happened for a reason. He carried a strange sense of peace about him. Determined to enjoy life, despite living by the seat of his pants most of the time, he compared himself to The Fool in the Tarot deck, always on the edge, stepping off the mountaintop, happy to take on the world at any moment.

I personally identified with him in a way I had never experienced before, and have always considered him my first real friend and brother. Given that BJ was busying himself with newfound fatherhood, David and I in the beginning had a lot of time to hang out on our own.

A week after our meeting, I discovered that David was living with an older guy who had carved holes in his bathroom walls so he could watch young boys shower and pee. I insisted that David come and stay at my mother's and bunk on the couch for as long as he liked, so he moved in with us the following week, and we became inseparable for the next year and a half—for better or worse.

THE ANGRY ATHEIST

Unlike David, I didn't believe that everything happens for a reason. I was extremely angry at God and blamed Him for all I had gone through in my short life. In childhood, I'd received great comfort from relying on God, but in my late teens I'd grown skeptical and come to believe that God, like everything else, was just something I had made up in my head. I bounced back and forth between belief and atheism, striking back at God by denying His very existence. Looking back, I think I felt abandoned by God.

My mother had her own relationship with God. Explaining that she had no need of a church, she would often just look up and say, "Hey, pal," and then say out loud what was bothering her. Considering her lifestyle, history, and the fact that she often drank herself into oblivion, it was easy for me to dismiss her faith as empty words and view her as one of the most hopeless individuals I had met. Still, her relationship with God was undeniable, and when she was sober, she often tried to offer hope and compassion to deter my rages.

It is said that our personalities are formed by the time we are three and depending on those formative years, you either view the world as safe or not. Confused by much of what I had experienced in my childhood, I spent a lot of time feeling completely lost and stressed. I'd been destroyed by childhood caretakers and often wondered what I had done to God to deserve what I had gone through.

What I'd been told about my mother had not been the real story, as my father had also destroyed her. She too had endured his beatings. As we discussed my conception and birth, it dawned on me that my mother had been just one more person my father had used, abused, and discarded when she no longer served his purposes. Although a product of her own life choices, she had been as broken by my father as we all had, while he'd come out smelling like a rose. My mother, siblings, and I were left to suffer the consequences of his behavior, and the injustice of it fueled my rage.

Though estranged from my father and his family, I still suffered mentally and emotionally from their abuse. Picking up where my father and stepmother left off, my brain constantly undermined me, looping over and over again about how worthless I was. Feeling that the world could rot and me along with it, I spent a great deal of time feeling sorry for myself, unable to find a way out of my predicament. Battling such anger all the time was exhausting, and I often had headaches and body tension along with panic attacks, all the while blaming God.

David had an interesting saying about *evil* being *live* spelled backwards, and he thought the stress I was force-feeding myself was an example of it. I adamantly disagreed, declaring that evil was a living, breathing force that compelled people to perpetrate terrible atrocities upon each other.

Whether or not the evil in Omaha was natural or necessary, I am unable to determine, but it certainly was pervasive, and I was about to get another bittersweet taste of the darkness I thought I'd buried with my past.

SOMETHING WICKED THIS WAY COMES

BJ finally met David and we all started hanging out together. It could be said that both were an incredibly bad influence on me, but having friends my own age was good. With BJ's connections and my money from Dick, and tips from Stars, we smoked countless bags of pot.

Smoking marijuana for the first time in my life, it was like nothing I had ever experienced. Getting high released me from the stress I constantly felt and energized me in a way I wasn't used to. Thus began a routine of "waking and baking" with David and BJ, much to the dismay of my mother.

"Drugs and friends, they come in that order," David would say as he puffed on BJ's bong, and we would all laugh, not realizing how true his insight would turn out to be. Never considering the consequences of what we were doing, David and I allowed BJ to constantly press us to try new experiences and we were happy to oblige.

Acid was also in heavy supply at the time, and BJ pushed us to try it. I held out for months, but with both David and BJ urging me, I finally broke down one night and tried it. Acid for me was a religious experience. It pried open pathways in my mind and I fell for hours into the grace of God.

BJ explained that the experience vastly depended upon the environment and the company you're keeping when high. Not once did I equate what we were doing with what was done to me as a child, so I guess he was right. The three of us just spent hours talking about God and man's relationship to the universe, high on both drugs and life.

David was the most adept thief I have ever known, and he began to teach me the finer nuances of shoplifting. Sometimes we had contests of who could steal more and would go all over town stealing from business after business. Once my mother realized that I was stealing all my new toys, she became enraged and warned us that we were going to end up in jail, but David and I just laughed and disregarded her good advice while planning our next escapade.

The best way to steal is out in the open, so I became accustomed to simply walking out of the stores with merchandise: answering machines, clothes, books. It didn't really matter; I just took whatever I wanted. Once, falling behind in our contest of who could steal more in a day, I walked into a bookstore and left with six hardcover books. My abilities didn't compare with David's, however; his crowning achievement in thievery was an entire Bose sound system.

My mother's apartment became Grand Central Station, with new friends and acquaintances constantly coming and going. My lonely existence had finally come to an end, or so I thought at the time, and all the activity seemed to slow down my mother's drinking.

Mark Andersen came around often on his motorcycle and took us for rides. He didn't approve of the drugs or the stealing, but he generally minded his own business and kept quiet. In his late forties to early fifties, Mark felt young again when he was around us and enjoyed our company as much as we enjoyed his, and we spent many hours talking and laughing. In some ways, he was a father figure for us.

Later, he introduced us to his friend Walter Carlson. Quiet, shy, polite, and middle-aged, Walt was pretty docile next to Mark's outgoing personality and blended in with the wallpaper whenever he came over. He lived in the basement of his parent's house over by Crossroads Mall in midtown. Neither of them realized that knowing us would mean their future downfall.

On weekdays, BJ, David, and I got high and hung out, sharing in a way that only comes with youth, pouring out our souls in hours of talk, seeking solace in the comfort each offered the other. Since none of us had it easy growing up, we all had tales to tell. David was somewhat secretive about his childhood, saying only that his parents didn't like him because he was gay and spent most of their time avoiding him. Ostracized in school, he had grown up as the weird kid, something BJ and I understood very well.

Unlike David, BJ was incredibly forthcoming about his childhood. Growing up with an alcoholic father and an overbearing, narcissistic, beautiful sociopath mom, he had found himself in a lifetime of situations that no person should have to experience. Once while drunk, his father had awakened him and demanded that he do a back flip for his friends. BJ broke his shoulder blade in the process, but neither of his parents took him to the hospital so it mended badly.

His mother, always in quest of a new husband, had a history of marrying and divorcing men. BJ bounced between the two until his mother remarried a man who didn't like him. BJ's life had been one letdown after another. Despite a gay childhood, he'd married his high school sweetheart, his only hold on stability.

He bragged about being able to get into the bars at fifteen due to his "connections," and was a compendium of information concerning the ins and outs of the Omaha gay scene.

The prospect of his friends getting me into the bars early should have been a waving red flag for me, but although I sensed a hidden darkness in BJ, I dismissed it. Our weekends were spent on the go, hanging out, socializing, and dancing. Neither Mark nor Walt ever came dancing with us, but they eagerly soaked up the stories we had to tell. Getting high and going down onto The Run around nine o'clock at night and hanging out before after-hours opened became customary on weekends. Finally feeling as if I was beginning to fit in, I started to allow myself to enjoy life for a while.

When Dick Bishop returned from Hawaii and asked me to start my cleaning position at his mansion, I wasn't all that anxious to begin. Hanging out with David and BJ had become as addictive as the drugs we were imbibing, probably because I'd never had friends and so I was co-dependent when it came to our camaraderie. BJ suggested he had a way for me to make money without having to work, but my mother insisted that I take the job, Dick being her friend and all.

I would soon learn that both BJ and my mother wanted the same thing: to pimp me out. They needn't have worried, however, as I was soon to discover just how small Omaha really was and how tightly wrapped in my past my present and future were to become.

6

A PEDERAST'S PLAYGROUND

The summer of 1986 was a bold time for those involved in nefarious activities in the Omaha area, and the party was going fast and hard.

The arrest of scapegoat John Joubert meant the "satanic panic" bullet had been successfully dodged, so Omaha again had become a free-for-all of anything goes. Working for Dick meant coming up to speed on how true this was. All I knew about Dick was that he'd been my mother's business partner and family friend who had struck out on his own and left my mother behind.

His house was an over-the-top Victorian, every corner of every over-decorated room filled with expensive eye candy that never allowed the mind to relax, and cleaning his house gave me a clear impression as to how wealthy the man was. I wasn't allowed upstairs where he was renting rooms to bikers he knew, but I cleaned the rest of the house and the pool, which was vaguely shaped like a penis and balls, supposedly in honor of its owner.

Dick was a voracious sex fiend constantly obsessing over his next lay and talking about it incessantly. Small, thin, and aggressively effeminate, Dick was all hands when he addressed me, which bothered me no end though I pretended to laugh it off. My mother said it was how Dick was and that he meant no harm by it. However, after watching how he paraded around with bikers and pubescent boys, I began to suspect there was more to him than met the eye. I never saw any money change hands, but I suspected sex for hire, which made me very uncomfortable.

One day Dick came into the house with an extremely attractive biker who lived upstairs, asking me to come into his bedroom where he was hanging curtains to talk about my wages. Mom's binge for a week or so had stressed me and I was not sleeping well so Dick offered to give me a massage. I declined until Dick pointed out that his friend was also in the room, assuring me I had nothing to worry about.

Against my better judgment, I complied, lying down on his pedestal bed a good four feet off the floor while he sat fully clothed beside me and began massaging my shoulders. As I began to relax, he started down my back, commenting on how tense my muscles were. Finally, using the excuse that he wanted to massage my lower back, he straddled me. Feeling his erect penis through my clothes as he began rubbing his erection on me, I panicked, throwing him off me and onto the floor, knocking the wind out of him in the process.

Scared he might be injured, both his friend and I rushed to his side. I apologized, convinced I had overreacted, and implored him to forgive me, that I was young, didn't know, and so on. Still struggling to catch his breath, he looked up at me and hissed, "When you were six, you were going on twenty-six." He didn't want to hear any excuses about my age.

Taken aback, I stood up. Still furious, he told me, "You are nothing like your older brother." Noticing my befuddlement, he smiled coldly and said, "I was fucking your brother at ten years old. We all were, and you know what? He loved it."

I left immediately, angry and confused over what I had just heard. My mother had lied to me; Dick was one of the people from the past I had spent years telling myself didn't exist. But instead of talking to my mother, I did what I always did at such times: I kept it to myself.

It is amazing how secrets can eat a person up, and this one was a difficult secret to accept. I told myself that none of it was true although I kept my distance from Dick, a self-admitted pedophile. Years later, I asked my brother about it, and he confirmed what Dick had said, but told me that if I told anyone he would kill me.

Sensing that something bad had transpired between Dick and me, my mother was silent. At times, she would catch me looking at her and ask what I was thinking but, just beginning to understand the anger my older siblings held toward her, I would just smile to avoid the argument that would have ensued had I said what was really on my mind.

DICK BISHOP

Interior Designer Richard Bishop Dies in Hawaii, April 7, 1988, *Omaha World-Herald*: Richard "Dick" Bishop, a prominent Omaha interior designer and former amateur bull rider known for his lavish parties, died Monday evening in Honolulu. ... Bishop was a frequent organizer of political and social gatherings that came to be known as "happenings."

Once again jobless and broke and tired of hearing my mother bitch about how she was sick of supporting me, I told BJ I was ready to meet the "friends" he said could help me out. A journey of a thousand miles begins with one small step, and until recovery, abuse survivors are drawn to putting themselves in re-victimizing situations, which was definitely true for the three of us.

Especially for BJ and me, given how we both had suffered major childhood ritualistic sexual abuse, prostitution looked like the norm at the time. I felt there was no other option, given that I couldn't keep a job. BJ assured David and me that it was no big deal; there was big money to be made from the men in town who were constantly seeking the company of young boys and willing to pay for it. I was completely unaware; the Devil was about to exact a price.

THE DEVIL'S HANDIWORK

BJ was running boys for a man named Alan Baer, a wealthy businessman eager to meet young men such as us. Explaining, BJ assured me that my being of age was a big plus in the mix as Baer had just gotten busted for soliciting sex with minors and was being extra cautious about age. He'd skated through the charge with a $500 fine, but was still paranoid of another Omaha "witch hunt."

BJ hustled boys in the Old Market and hooked up with Boys Town boys as they came into Omaha via the Greyhound bus station every Saturday morning. He befriended them, as he had me, and then introduced them to Alan for a commission. His own mother had brought him to Alan at a young age, and he'd become a courier at fourteen, his reward being access to bars by fifteen.

Referring to himself as a Baer Boy, BJ expressed how nice it was to have a powerful man who could do things for him, and assured us that if we let him Alan would do the same for us. All BJ had to do was make the phone call. His talk scared me, and I backed out. The easy money was intriguing, but I wasn't yet ready to take on the role of pimp.

David, on the other hand, was all for it. Always jumping in feet first, he was ready for the next adventure. To him, the danger sounded like just one more experience to add to his growing list of dangers. I stood my ground, but then as usual relented and agreed to meet another of BJ's friends just to test the waters.

Peer pressure coupled with our usual competition made it hard to continue saying no, and I was afraid they would leave me behind and all alone again, so I ignored the little inner voice telling me that I was going in the wrong direction. No one held a gun to my head, but I was always conflicted and desperately afraid of loneliness. Still, I had a sense that I would regret what I was about to do.

BJ made a phone call and I hustled my mother out of the apartment to her friend Aunt Ruth's across the street so I could have some alone time with my "gentleman caller." My mother was on a walker at the time and getting around wasn't that easy, so she asked me what I was up to. Assuring her that nothing was going on, she still managed to overhear the three of us talking, when she, hobbling across the street, began yelling at the top of her lungs, "I am not living in a brothel!"

Horrified, I tried to quiet her ranting by saying I would only be an hour or so, at which she looked at me and said quietly, "You have no idea what you are getting into," then continued on to Aunt Ruth's.

I would like to say that it was an awful experience and it all ended there, but I can't. Michael Van was about 5 feet 9, thin, dark hair and mustache, and one of the hottest guys I'd ever met. BJ and David went downstairs to BJ's apartment and left us alone.

I was nervous at first, but the encounter ended up being a really hot sex session resulting in mutual masturbation. He gave me $100 and told me I would have gotten more had he been able to fuck me and that he'd like to meet me again sometime. Having no interest in anal intercourse, I waited for him to leave, then went downstairs to give the other two the details. My mother returned later, poured a drink, and stayed drunk for the next week and a half.

THE DEVIL HIMSELF

I am now able to introduce the notorious Alan Baer, a man who, in many ways, would change my life forever.

My first impression of him was right out of *Planet of the Apes* because he resembled a small primate, and yet he was one of the most intelligent men I had ever met. He picked me up at my mother's apartment, and we drove around in his black two-seater sports car, talking about my education, my background, and, amusingly enough, my family.

A consummate game player, he kept me off guard with questions and had a way of getting information out of me without my even knowing it by using flattery and coy knowing smiles. He made me feel comfortable; the ride was fun and the man intriguing, however, when he asked me how my father was, I should have known that he too was somehow connected to the sinister happenings of my childhood. Noting that I was estranged and unwilling to talk about him, Alan changed the subject.

Alan Baer's apartment at Twin Towers.

We drove into an affluent, old-money area of Omaha called Fairacres, and he pointed out a large mansion with a huge party tent in the backyard. He said he was having a party and went into great detail about the work involved in throwing such a gala.

Later, I would discover it was all a lie. He did live in Fairacres, but that particular mansion wasn't his. Not knowing this at the time, I was suitably impressed.

When he dropped me off at my mother's, he handed me $50 for the time I'd spent with him and asked if it would be okay to call me in the future. I gave him my number, got out of the car, went into the house, and told BJ and David everything.

A week later, I agreed to meet Alan at his Twin Towers apartment eight blocks from my mother's apartment. I knocked on 2J, and he opened the door in shorts, sweating profusely. For an older man, he was in great shape, thanks to the veritable gym he'd fashioned in the living room.

It dawned on me that 2J was his run-down bachelor pad, and he explained it was a great getaway from his workday. Alan had a way of coming off as just a weird old guy who was extremely charming in his strange way, so I often dismissed his behavior as mere eccentricities. But they weren't: he was a real snake in the grass with a motive for everything he said and did.

Walking on his treadmill the whole time, he asked about BJ and David and what we did when we hung out. Happy to answer his questions, I told him the basic situation at my mother's house. He was a complete gentleman, never once suggesting sex. When our time came to an end, he handed me $250, walked me to the door, and told me he would be in contact.

My mother kept trying to convince me to steer clear of what she surmised was prostitution and to go get a real job. I thought her objections were hypocritical, given that she'd done the same thing herself, but since then I've learned that the best lessons to be learned are from people who have made the same mistakes.

Over the next few weeks, I met Alan a few times. We always conversed as he drove around in his car. He liked my vocabulary and the fact that I was well read, and we often spoke of politics and what was happening in the world. Getting paid every time we met, sometimes up to $500, I started to genuinely like the guy against my better judgment. So by the time he actually asked to have sex, I was a willing participant.

His penthouse apartment on top of the Brandeis building downtown was in stark contrast to the Twin Towers apartment just east of the Mutual of Omaha headquarters. Lavishly decorated, with dozens of mounted animal heads on the wall, it was elegant in its masculinity and incredibly impressive. Nervous and eager to get sex over with, I asked if I could use the bathroom, at which time he told me that he wanted me to shower as well. Having just taken a shower before I walked down, I thought it was a strange request but, in no position to disagree, I simply asked where the towels were.

Considering David's experience with the pervert and the holes in the wall, you'd think I would have been nervous about being filmed. In retrospect, I realize that I probably was, and that the whole thing was some weird sort of setup, but at the time I was too nervous at the prospect of what I would have to do to think much about it.

Alan ended up giving me a blow job on the balcony of his penthouse. I was uncomfortable with the buildings around us and the people working in them so I couldn't get into it. My lackluster performance ended twenty minutes later, at which point we got dressed. He handed me $500 and showed me to the elevator.

The next day, an acquaintance of mine and my mother's named Andrew told Alan, at my mother's insistence, that I was emotionally unstable and dangerous. When Alan told me what Andrew had said and that he had decided it was best that we end contact, I became enraged and returned home to find Andrew and my mother sitting down to a bowl of hot chili. It was hot as hell in my mother's house, in the dead of summer, and Andrew had taken off his shirt and was sitting bare-chested on the couch, blowing on his chili to cool it off.

I flew into a rage I couldn't control, as if I mentally moved aside and let my body take control. It was like I was someone else, watching myself from afar. Grabbing a knife in the kitchen, I put it to Andrew's throat, warning him that if he moved, I would cut him from ear to ear. Reacting, he spilled hot chili all over his bare chest and began sobbing, scared and in pain.

Mom stood up on her walker and begged me to put the knife down while I demanded to know what he had told Alan. All I can remember is my mother pleading and Andrew sobbing, and a female friend of mine who had come with me to the apartment urged me to leave with her and stop the madness.

I told Andrew that if I ever saw him again, I would hurt him, then put the knife down and walked out. Andrew left and never returned, and my mother and I never once spoke about what had transpired. Terrified by my own rage, I did my best to forget the episode, but every time I looked in the mirror, I saw the Devil and felt like a psychopath—exactly what my mother had chosen to warn Alan of.

My business relationship with Alan was over, but his influence on my life was just beginning, in ways that I never could have imagined.

THE PRINCE OF POWER

Back in the mid-1980s, Thomas Thompson wrote a book called *Celebrity* in which three friends come together, form a friendship, and then collapse—a foreshadowing of what was about to happen to BJ, David, and me. We had even adopted the names from the book: BJ the Prince of Temptation was always tempting us to go one step further; David the Prince of Charms enchanted everyone with his personality and laughter; and me, the Prince of Power who never quite fit the name, given that I wasn't as good looking as David or BJ and lacked their grace, charm, and sexual prowess. Both could get any guy they desired and left me in the dust when it came to sex.

Nor was I that great of a friend, given my few boundaries and no idea of what friendship really was. I was demanding and unforgiving and when I became jealous of their relationship, I began spending a lot of time away from them, especially after BJ introduced David to Alan Baer and they began hanging together—BJ still a favorite of Alan's.

BJ and his wife and new baby were busy in their own chaos, as was David, with his downtown sex parties where all the sex, money, and drugs flowed. He had quickly become enmeshed in the world that my mother had wisely, it turned out, declared off limits to me.

I began hanging out in East Omaha where Mark lived. He and Walt and I would have cookouts by Carter Lake and I'd help mow Mark's lawn. It was fun associating with them, laughing about nothing. Walt was slowly coming out of his shell, and the three of us talked about science and history.

Meanwhile, BJ's chaos was growing. He was drinking heavily, and like my mother, he was an incredibly mean drunk. One night he terrorized the whole apartment, attacking his wife, chasing a neighbor and her five children out of their own apartment after he had chased his wife into it. Everyone somehow ended up hiding in my mother's apartment while I tried to deal with the madman in the hallway that wanted his baby girl but was too intoxicated and out of control to be trusted with her.

He ran down the hallway and slammed his body weight into our back door over and over as I stood on the other side, pressed against the kitchen counter and bracing the door with my legs. My mother held his daughter in the living room, along with a knife that she planned to use on him if he succeeded in breaking through, while everyone else hid in her bedroom. Finally exhausted, he sped off in his car and totaled it, and had his daughter been with him, she would probably have died. David slept through the entire drama, not wanting to deal with the chaos.

Angry with both pals for leaving me behind to live in the fast lane, I felt things spiraling out of control and began further distancing myself from them. Shoplifting sprees were becoming a thing of the past for me, as I was tired of feeling like a criminal all the time and seemed incapable of keeping a grip on anything. Owing to the influx of strangers going through our apartment, we were constantly getting robbed.

I was jealous of the fun the two seemed to be having and so I tried to control David as if I owned him, meanwhile blaming BJ for bringing Alan into our lives and conspiring to take David from me. Our three-way relationship became more and more strained as David fought for his independence. It felt as if everything was slipping through my fingers.

That Christmas was the last really nice time we would have as a group, as if a *grace* fell upon us to help us get along. David's parents had tempted him with a trip to Hawaii and then dashed his hopes at the last minute. Hearing of this, my sister Cindy duplicated everything she was giving me and sent it from Florida in time for Christmas, making David very happy. BJ and his wife were getting along, and no one was drinking.

The calm before the storm, it was the last time we would be together as friends. A Judas in the group, one would run, one would die, and Mark and Walt would spend years of their life in prison.

7

ALL THE KING'S MEN AND THE NAUGHTY BAER BOYS

The gay community in 1987 was extremely ostentatious; with two well-known groups of "kept" individuals called "Baer Boys" and "King's Men," nicknames earned by those being kept by two rich men in town, Alan Baer and Larry King. King, a middle-aged African American who was currently serving as president of Franklin Credit Union, was also a well-known Republican who sang at President Ronald Reagan's inaugural ball while at the same time bilking the credit union out of $40 million.

THE RISE AND FALL OF THE FRANKLIN CREDIT UNION

Franklin Credit Union Expands Headquarters, *Omaha World-Herald,* June 18, 1985 (metro section): The Franklin credit union was founded in 1968 by a Franklin Street neighborhood group concerned about the lack of financial institutions in Omaha's north side. ... With the help of its current manager, Lawrence E. King Jr., the fledgling institution avoided closing and attracted grants from such organizations as the national Presbyterian and Methodist churches. ... The credit union official said among the people attending Wednesday's ceremony will be Harold W. Andersen, president of *The World-Herald*.

Chronology of Events Linked to Franklin Credit Union, July 25, 1990, *Omaha World-Herald* (metro, p. 14): [On] Nov. 4, 1988: The National Credit Union Administration, a federal regulatory agency, closed Omaha's Franklin Community Federal Credit Union because it was engaging in "unsafe and unsound practices." Lawrence E. King, Jr., Franklin's top officer, said the NCUA's allegation came as "a complete surprise." Nov. 11, 1988: Although Franklin's records showed the credit union had assets of $2.5 million and liabilities of $2 million, the NCUA said $30 million [later revised on Dec. 1, 1988, to $39 million] was missing. [On November 20, 1988, the newspaper revealed that King drove a $69,300 white Mercedes, often chartered jets and rode in rented limos. He rented a house in Washington, D.C., for $5,000 a month and gave lavish parties. His annual salary at Franklin was $16,200.] [On December 19, 1988, state Senator Ernie Chambers said the state foster care review board and the Omaha Police Department were sitting on a report alleging children had been abused. Later a state legislature-appointed committee was to investigate the Franklin failure and related child-abuse allegations.]

Judge Will Tell Grand Jury: Probe All Aspects of Case, February 20, 1990, *Omaha World-Herald* (metro, p. 1): The Douglas County [Omaha] grand jury will have no restrictions in its investigation of child abuse allegations and other matters arising out of the Franklin Credit Union case, Presiding Judge James Buckley said Tuesday. ... The county's judges called a grand jury to look into allegations of child abuse somehow related to Omaha's failed Franklin Community Federal Credit Union.

Panel Ends 82-Day Look at Franklin Report: Exonerates Prominent Omahans, July 24, 1990, *Omaha World-Herald* (metro, p. 1): A Douglas County grand jury Tuesday sharply criticized some state officials and others who made accusations in the Franklin Credit Union case. It indicted three people and cleared a number of prominent Omahans of sexual wrongdoing. The grand jury debunked many of the rumors that have surrounded the 1988 failure of the credit union. ... "We found no credible evidence of child sexual abuse, interstate transportation of minors, drug trafficking or participation in a pornography ring," the grand jury said.

Three Indicted: Jury Sees 'Hoax,' Baer Facing Two Counts of Pandering, July 24, 1990, *Omaha World-Herald* (metro, p. 1): A Douglas County grand jury indicted ... Alan Baer on two counts of pandering ... Baer was accused of paying adult men for sexual services. ... Baer's attorney, Steve Seline of Omaha, said Tuesday that Baer is "pleased and gratified" that the grand jury "vindicated" him from any rumors of sexual abuse of children.

Alan Baer had the vast fortune of his (department store) Brandeis family at his disposal. His foundation supported arts and culture in Omaha, and he owned several successful businesses, as well.

Gay men constantly pandered to Alan and Larry, hoping to find favor with them for money and position.

Intricately involved in the gay community at the time, Alan and Larry funded lavish charity galas in the bars and hosted even bigger parties at their homes. "King's Men" often provided muscle for Larry's enterprises and parties, and young black males acted as bodyguards and bouncers.

Being a Baer Boy or King's Man was prestigious. Along with money, it often meant an apartment, a car, and being invited to all the best parties with all the best drugs. The tradeoff was that Baer Boys and King's Men were expected to entertain guests at the parties and make sure everyone was having a good time— plentiful drugs, full drinks, noses full of coke, and, of course, young boys and girls. Trips were granted to the chosen, such as when Alan wanted to take BJ to Florida with him.

However, involvement with Alan and Larry was risky. Displeasing them in any way meant finding yourself out on the street. King's Men came out onto the street to find their cars missing, repossessed by the very men who had given them in the first place. There were always strings. I've heard it said that if you give a man enough rope, he will hang himself, and this was especially true of those who worked for these arrogant, boastful, and temperamental men who enjoyed watching people squirm. Fun could just as well turn to pain at a moment's notice.

For people like Alan, Larry, Dick Bishop, and Peter Citron—a local columnist for the town's only newspaper, the *Omaha World-Herald*, who eventually went to jail for pedophilia—Omaha was a virtual playground. It hosted the rich, the connected, and the demented. ~~Robert Wadman~~

Rich men were making heaps of off-the-books money with drugs and prostitution, and though plenty of people knew what was going on because it was blatant and in your face, since local law enforcement such as Omaha Police Chief Robert Wadman was in on it as well, there was nothing anyone could do or say.

In the beginning, I went with BJ and David to the impressive, ostentatious parties at Larry King's penthouse in Twin Towers and Alan Baer's Brandeis mansion, among other places. Sparing absolutely no expense, Larry and Alan threw party after party. Catered food of shrimp and lobster was never-ending as was the open bar.

Given their powerful connections, you never knew who you would see or what you were likely to see them doing. Bathroom coke breaks were the norm. Publicly, Alan and Larry were dead set against drugs, but everyone knew what was going on as groups of people would hang out in the bathrooms filling their noses. It was the 1980s and everyone was doing it, so it didn't seem bad or wrong, and the money being made off coke was incredible.

The big reason I began declining BJ's and David's invitations was that kids were at the parties. Although child prostitution wasn't out in the open, everyone had to know what was happening, and people seemed to overlook almost anything if there is enough money involved. There was always a free bar, so it seemed easy enough to order another drink and look away, figuring the always-white boys and girls ages nine or ten to sixteen wouldn't be there if they didn't want to be.

It all began to break apart around the first of the year in 1987 when rumors of an investigation into Larry's Franklin Credit Union began to circulate. Investigations into children had already begun, so people were whispering about a bad moon rising, which put a damper on the never-ending party that had been raging for generations.

The question was who was going to get stuck with the bill? Being the men they were, Alan and Larry had quite a few enemies looking for any reason to nail them, and kids and money were used to bring them down.

Kevin Dobson

THE UNRAVELING BEGINS

ven with the arrest of John Joubert for the unrelated yet gruesome child killings, the problems associated with child abuse and prostitution didn't go away. The gay community was abuzz with rumors of satanic practices, child pornography and snuff films, and a myriad of other crimes that had been taking place in the gay bars and Old Market area.

The Iran-Contra affair was just hitting the news, and some knew that Omaha was involved with importing Contra cocaine. A local dealer in town by the name of Kevin Dobson was connected with Dick Bishop and his Hell's Angels and had been bragging for years how he'd been running guns to Nicaragua and shipping cocaine back, which was why Omaha was the coke-rich area it was.

Offutt Air Force Base was accused of being involved in secret government projects torturing and sexually abusing children in the area. A few years later this would all hit the media, and a circus would ensue, but not before things started to get ugly in Omaha.

In fact, the summer of 1987 was when what I call Project Clean-up really began. A great deal of power can be brokered from a campaign of fear. An epidemic of "suicides" that summer made being a Baer Boy a dangerous pursuit. Several of the apparent suicides opted for the method of wrapping plastic around their faces, although it was never explained exactly how or why someone would choose to die that way.

Needless to say, fear stalked the gay community. Meanwhile, the suicides were not reported in the media nor tracked in any way, so the community at large was unaware of these numerous deaths while those in the gay community who knew anything quickly learned to keep their mouths shut.

Despite the fact that many of the people involved were my mother's best friends, I adamantly denied that what was happening had any connection to my family's past, but I was soon to be awakened in a way that would force me to pull my head out of the sand.

It started when I went with acquaintances to a funeral after some Baer Boy shot himself in the head on the promise that hot gay guys would be there and I could possibly find a date. Sitting down in the pew, I scanned the crowd, later opening the memorial program to see if I recognized the deceased, at which point my stomach lurched.

I'd known Charlie (we called him CB) Rogers when I was fifteen. We'd been introduced by my uncle's daughter who would later humiliate me by saying in a room filled with my father's family that since Charlie was gay and I was gay, it just seemed natural to match us up.

Back then, Charlie lived about a half mile from my grandmother's condo, and I would walk to his apartment when we came to Omaha and visited my grandmother and hang out with him as the only openly gay man I knew. In his mid-twenties then, 5 feet 9 with sandy blond hair, a mustache, and a tan, he was like some hot 1970s porn star, and I found him fascinating as he also proved to be good in bed.

He took me to The Hollywood bar and showed me the dark, scary, and incredibly creepy dungeon setup in the basement. Scared, I had demanded to leave immediately. When the town tore the bar down and built the parking garage over it, I said good riddance.

After being narced out by my cousin that I was doing the wild thing with an older man, my father squelched the relationship with Charlie. Sitting now at Charlie's funeral, I knew that he was too supremely narcissistic to ever kill himself, and I got an uneasy feeling that not all was as it seemed. I left the funeral shaken. Knowing that he was considered to be high in the ranks of the naughty Baer Boys and King's Men, I figured Alan and his associates were cutting their losses.

> Suicide Victim Received Gifts, February 26, 1989, *Omaha World-Herald* (page 1A): There was the $2,810 deerskin coat the receipt said was purchased by "Larry King" at an exclusive shop in California and shipped to Charlie Rogers in Omaha. And the 18-karat gold bracelet inscribed to "Charlie" from "The Boss." … There was no doubt that Charlie Rogers, a 29-year-old lawn-service operator, was a friend of and received gifts from Lawrence E. King Jr., chief executive of Franklin Community Federal Credit Union, said Douglas County Sheriff's Capt. Robert Tramp. … Well-built, likable Charlie Rogers was one of a number of young men—usually white and in their 20s—for whom King bought gifts and on whom he bestowed favors, said three former associates of the one-time credit-union chief. … Besides the Max, [Rogers] also had worked as a bartender at the old Hollywood bar at 14th

and Harney Streets … Rogers' family members say he had told them several weeks before his death [by a shot to the head with a .12-gauge Ithaca shotgun he owned] that if anything happened to him they should contact Deputy Douglas County Attorney Sigler [who commented: "I don't have a comment."].

It was also during Project Clean-up that Mark and Walt were charged with crimes against children, which I found to be ridiculous. Mark had invited three hustlers to spend the night on his living room floor and had either inadvertently or intentionally touched one boy's butt. The boy's parents tried to extort money out of Mark and failed, then turned to the police and pressed charges. Harold Andersn

Suddenly, the *Omaha World-Herald,* whose owner Harold Andersen was reportedly involved in the Larry King/Franklin Credit Union scandal, began touting Walt, the shyest person I'd ever met, as the Pied Piper of Pornography, and Mark and Walt were proclaimed as menaces to society by the local media. Mark told me that he would just try to keep his distance while his troubles played out, but everything was turning upside down, and I didn't know what to think or whom to trust.

Besides Mark's withdrawal, things had cooled off among David and BJ and me. Both had been deeply involved with Alan Baer and had disassociated themselves from me, probably due to secrets I knew nothing about.

Despairing over my failed friendships, I once again found myself alone, miserable, and angry with no job, no money, and no options. My mother pressed me to leave town for a while and visit my sister Cindy, and her prodding irritated me as I saw it as yet another example of how she was trying to control my life in her newfound role as my mother.

Now I realize that she was saving my life by sending me away from a situation she was afraid would somehow envelope me. Confused and a bit scared, I finally gave in and let her buy me a bus ticket to Florida. Looking back I see that more was going on in Omaha than even I was aware of at the time, and my decision to leave probably saved my life.

I packed a suitcase, hugged my mom, got on the Greyhound bus and headed for my big sister's, believing I was leaving all the chaos occurring around me behind. I couldn't have been more wrong.

THE SUMMER OF LOSS

The summer began well. Within a week of arriving in Florida, I found a job at a local resort as a waiter in a barbeque restaurant right off the beach and was able to move out of my sister's right away into an apartment also off the beach.

My relationship with Cindy had always been tenuous. She'd saved my neck more than once while she and her family lived with me and my father and our stepmother, but she could also be vindictive and vicious. A game player to the max, she was expert at setting people up.

My sister's husband, Ralph, was an extremely overweight, loud, and obnoxious man who had always disliked our family. Her children, who were close in age to me, were obnoxious game players themselves, with drugs and beer and up until four in the morning party lifestyles.

Needless to say I didn't see much of them. Occasionally, I hung with people from work, but most often I wrote in my journal on the beach, watching storms roll in like clockwork every afternoon, imagining I was watching God on the ocean, as the wind and rain picked up until I was surrounded by lightning and thunder and had to leave the area. A daily religious experience, the ocean spoke to me in a way that touched me deeply, comforting me, helping me to feel normal. I excelled at my job and was promoted from waiter to front room manager, and in many ways it was the best few months I'd ever had, although the peace was not to last long.

My mother had taken to calling me with concern about David and what he was telling her. Sworn to secrecy, she wouldn't tell me exactly what he was saying—only that he was in over his head with Alan Baer. David and I weren't speaking at this point, having ended our friendship. I was concerned but had no idea what to do.

So I tested the waters and wrote a letter to BJ, using him as a sounding board as I explained what I planned to say to David, hoping that he might give a heads-up to David. I had reached the point of being big enough to say I was wrong, and often relished the image of David forgiving me, enabling us to work things through and resume a friendship.

I will never forget that next week, the week David was murdered, at the tender age of nineteen. With the help of local media outlets, the problems regarding misdeeds in Omaha would magically disappear the same week.

Drunk off her ass and sobbing, my mother reached me by phone at work during a dinner rush. She'd been calling all over town looking for me. Her voice at a whisper, she said, "David was shot in the face and killed by his roommate."

Dropping the phone, I caught myself almost about to wail in a restaurant filled with people. I hung up on my mother and retreated to the back office, feeling as if my world had just come to an end, and I began to sob. Then the phone rang again. Thinking it was my mother calling back, I answered, "What do you want?" However, it was BJ.

"I wanted to be the person to tell you," was all he said. I thanked him, claiming I had to go, and hung up.

David died September 6, 1987, a little over a year and a half after we first met.

Having to buy a plane ticket two weeks in advance, I spent the next two weeks sobbing, waiting to fly back to Omaha to say goodbye to everyone in my life. Omaha media stories that week said David was killed by his roommate Mike James, for reasons unclear; John Joubert was convicted and sentenced to death; and Mark Andersen and Walt Carlson were convicted and sentenced to spend years in prison.

No real evidence linked Mark and Walt to any crime, but Omaha had become a circus dictating justice from a kangaroo court. The fact that the parents of the boy had tried to extort money from Mark before going to the police (which came out in court), was insufficient to save him and Walt from prison.

13 Charged in Porn Probe; Boys Taped, Debauched, December 19, 1985, *Omaha World-Herald* (metro): Omaha police began a roundup Thursday of 13 men facing a total of 99 charges coming from a six-week, citywide investigation into sexual exploitation of boys. [The list included Walter Carlson and Mark Andersen.]

Court Orders Trial in Sex Case, January 7, 1986, *Omaha World-Herald:* A 16-year-old boy testified Monday that he engaged in a sex act with Walter Carlson during the summer of 1984 after watching pornographic movies in Carlson's home.

Jury Told Boys Fabricated Reports of Sexual Assault, September 9, 1987, *Omaha World-Herald:* A 38-year-old Omaha man went to court Tuesday for the start of his trial on charges that he sexually assaulted 11-year-old boys in his home. Mark G. Andersen ... faces sexual assault charges involving three boys and five alleged sexual assaults in 1984 and 1985.

Jury in Sex-Assault Trial Hears Two Boys Testify, September 9, 1987, *Omaha World-Herald* (metro): A 13-year-old Omaha boy testified Wednesday that overnight visits with Mark G. Andersen usually included pornographic movies and sex. The boy, testifying in the second day of Andersen's trial on charges of sexual assault involving three boys, said Andersen made sexual advances during most of the 75 or 80 visits to Andersen's house in 1984 and 1985.

The media taught the public to associate these names and faces with crimes against children to thereby keep attention away from others who were truly guilty. Two men and a convicted killer were sacrificed as scapegoats upon which everyone could vent anger and frustration. Convicted by the media, it worked like magic. I couldn't believe it. And Alan Baer, guilty of pandering sex with minors and of so much more, only received a $500 fine by the same judicial system. The disparity enraged me.

Unable to work those two weeks, I was fired and felt my life was over. My despair was a living, breathing thing that dug its claws into my chest, and I often found myself doubled over on the floor, crying in fits for hours at a time.

Finally returning to Omaha, as my cab drove through downtown, I saw the same three hustlers who had put Mark and Walt in prison selling themselves down on The Run. Disgusted but not surprised, I stared at my hands until the cab pulled up to my mother's apartment. Drunk, my mother went on and on about David wanting to kick out the roommate who killed him. I never met Mike James (the roommate convicted of David's murder), nor did I ever want to, but soon I would have reason to be doubtful as to his guilt.

Unwilling to answer my questions about Alan Baer, my mother told me to "steer clear" of the situation. BJ, however, had been present at David's death and put it all into perspective for me, throwing me over the edge in the process.

Mike, David's roommate, had just gotten a job as a bank security guard complete with gun. Having no training or guidance in handling a gun, he would often playfully point the gun at people and pull the trigger repeatedly. The gun went off on the second click; the bullet entered David's cheek and blew out the back of his head, killing him instantly. Mike had been unaware that the gun was actually loaded. David had been laughing with him at the time, perhaps the only saving grace to a horrible situation.

BJ told me that David had been deep in debt to Alan Baer. Wanting to know what my mother had told me, he impressed upon me the importance of keeping my mouth shut. I asked him what he meant, and BJ looked me straight in the eye and explained that Mike had no idea the gun was loaded.

I paled, speechless. He went further to say that he had a gift for me from Alan Baer. Wanting nothing from the man, I demanded to know what it was. BJ walked to a cupboard and retrieved a red-spotted towel.

"This is what is left of David," he said, trying to hand me the towel of brain and bone fragments. Horrified, I began putting things together in way I hadn't before.

The fact that BJ would slip a bullet into a gun and set up another man to kill David for Alan was too much to handle, but in light of Mark and Walt being set up, it seemed sadly plausible. It was like living a nightmare, the blood and gore in the towel right before my eyes. David, Mark, Walt, gone, and only BJ and me left, with BJ involved in ways I didn't want to know. *Just live my life* was what I was being told to do, even though there was little left.

> David Klotz
>
> Argument Over Pet Led to Shooting: Slayer Given Four to Five Years in Prison, March 3, 1988, *Omaha World-Herald:* An 18-year-old Omaha man who fatally shot a friend during an argument about a pet ferret was sentenced Wednesday to four to five years in prison. ... Michael L. James said he would always regret having shot his best friend, 20-year-old David Klotz. ... James shot Klotz once in the head at the apartment they shared at 3913 Farnam St. Witnesses told police the Sept. 6 shooting occurred after James threatened to kill a pet ferret because it had fleas. ... James shot him after a struggle, authorities said. James used a revolver he had obtained for his job as a Wells Fargo security officer. He had been on the job about two weeks.

I flew back to Florida the next day in a state of shock while suffering a severe case of survivor guilt. I wondered why I'd been spared when everyone else had been taken. I was scared, confused, and totally alone. Once again I found myself in a soul desert where I would wander lost for the next several years.

Jobless and soon after homeless, I spent the next six months losing my mind and telling people that I had $521 million frozen in a bank account of drug money and that when I could get at it I would be rich. Although ridiculous, and constantly making a fool out of myself, I did what I did in order to escape the reality of what happened. Feeling responsible for David's death, I have often regretted sending BJ my letter, often wondering how things would have worked out had I not unintentionally narced out David the week before his death.

I spent no time with my sister and her family, instead fabricating a life that didn't exist. Some people actually believed me, and it was amazing the lengths at which they went to please. I got involved with an airman stationed at a nearby base and began weaving a fantastic web of lies to a man I was supposedly dating, feeling worse about myself daily. He was involved in his own chaos and wanted to get out of the service, so I convinced him to tell them that he was gay and dating me, not realizing that they would try to court martial him as a result.

Convinced that everything I touched turned to shit, I left in the middle of his disaster and called his family in hopes that they could help him. Two days after I left, they arrived and he called me, infuriated that his parents were sitting in his living room, and I confessed everything to him, or at least about the bogus $521 million dollars. Without a doubt, my life was out of control.

Returning to Omaha broken and downhearted, I made plans to go to the East Coast before the bus even pulled into the station. BJ had gone to Massachusetts to live with his mother. He was the only friend I had left. His marriage had been destroyed and his life overturned by guilt and regret over the "do or die" situation Alan had put him in. Having nothing left to lose, he bolted from Omaha.

Indeed most of the players left alive and not in jail scattered. Many feared being implicated in the upcoming investigation into Franklin. Even Dick picked up shop and went to Hawaii. In the end, only a handful of people would be implicated, and of those only a smaller handful would ever see jail. Neat and tidy, those really involved had dodged another bullet and, barring an act of God, would remain free to prosper while I spent years running from myself, trapped in an unspeakable hell.

THE FRANKLIN FIASCO

Public perception may have been manipulated and controlled, but there was still the matter of $40 million missing from the Franklin Credit Union. In 1988, the FBI finally raided and shut down Franklin and seized all of Larry King's files and property. Although there were allegations that he was running prostitutes into the White House and was involved in many nefarious acts concerning children, the only charges that stuck were fraud and those concerning fleecing the credit union. Larry King and Peter Citron were the only persons of influence to be implicated.

> Chronology of Events Linked to Franklin Credit Union, July 25, 1990, *Omaha World-Herald* (metro p. 1): May 19, 1989: A federal grand jury charged Lawrence E. King Jr. with 40 felony counts accusing him of crimes stemming from Franklin's financial failure.
>
> Franklin Attorneys Say Case Isn't Over, June 18, 1991, *Omaha World-Herald* (p. 1): Lawrence E. King Jr., ... and his wife, Alice

Ploche King, received maximum prison terms Monday ... for their roles in the diversion of $39 million from the Franklin treasury. King, 46, was given 15 years—three sentences of five years each to be served one after the other—for conspiracy, embezzlement and making false entries on the books of a federally insured institution.

'After King's Exposure, Public Believed Anything': Another View, March 2, 1992, *Omaha World-Herald* reprinting an article from *GQ*: Now credulousness became Larry King's enemy. Many of the same people who had believed in Saint Larry of the Credit Union came to believe, within a matter of months, in Larry the Monstrous, a pederast and a drug trafficker. Both personas were fictions, but both appealed to something deep in the public's imagination.

In the summer of 1988, the state attorney general received allegations of a child-abuse ring centering on Larry King. At the same time, a 15-year-old girl told an Omaha police officer that at age 9 she had been conscripted into a satanic cult in which older boys had forced her to have sex. They killed infants and children, she said.

Most of the focus fell on those I call the "famous three": Alisha Owen, Paul Bonacci, and Troy Boner. Involved in King's child prostitution rings, they came forth with allegations concerning Larry King, Alan Baer, and a slew of other wealthy businessmen, plus, most interestingly, Omaha's ex-police chief Robert Wadman.

Although their fantastic stories of abuse resembled mine, I knew Troy Boner to be a pathological liar and so discounted the entire exposé. After David's death and learning of BJ's complicity and Alan's involvement, I had little stomach for the whole mess, so I turned a blind eye, not giving a damn how it all played out. History chose to focus on just three victims when, in truth, there were thousands; and Larry King was put away when most of well-heeled Omaha was involved.

But the message to victims was loud and clear. The grand jury threw the book at Alisha Owen, sentencing her to twenty-seven years for perjury. This ended up including solitary, because she refused to recant that Robert Wadman, Omaha's police chief, was the father of the baby she had as a minor.

Naturally, Alisha's experience effectively silenced other victims who yearned to come forward. She was finally released in 2000. (As for the other two witnesses in the massive pedophilia conspiracy, Paul Bonacci won a $1 million lawsuit for damages, in 1999; Troy Boner was found dead in 2003.)

The media shredded the wild claims of the three victims and harped on their mental illness as the stories kept changing and becoming more bizarre, never considering that going through what they had gone through would make anyone crazy.

Backed by the False Memory Syndrome Foundation that had defeated similar allegations in California in 1983, the press vilified the three as liars, claiming they were conspirators in a carefully crafted hoax, though never expounding on who exactly could be behind such a hoax and why.

FALSE MEMORY SYNDROME FOUNDATION

The False Memory Syndrome Foundation is a nonprofit organization based in Philadelphia. Its goals are to seek the reasons for the spread of false memories that can be devastating to families, to work for ways to prevent it, and to help those affected by it and bring families into reconciliation.

Parents had been reporting that they had received phone calls and letters from their grown children accusing them of committing horrifying acts of abuse that allegedly had happened decades earlier. The Foundation's position is that families were being shattered when adult children suddenly claimed to have recovered repressed memories of childhood sexual abuse and incest.

The Foundation refers to a Random House dictionary definition of *false memory syndrome:* a psychological condition in which a person remembers events that *have not actually occurred.*

The website for the Foundation (fmsfonline.org) says, "Some of our memories are true, some are a mixture of fact and fantasy, and some are false—whether those memories seem to be continuous or seem to be recalled after a time of being forgotten or not thought about."

The controversy is how to distinguish between true and false memories, and the Foundation says the only way to distinguish the difference is by external corroboration.

The British documentary *Conspiracy of Silence* was supposed to air on the Discovery channel in 1994 but was pulled that day. It too addressed only the three victims and major players in the scandal, saying nothing of entrenched crime in Omaha and at Offutt Air Force Base. The documentary is now available on YouTube.

Police Say Bonacci Told of Molestation, Then 'Embellished,' August 9, 1990, *Omaha World-Herald* (p. 18): After being jailed for fondling boys, Paul Bonacci began telling police that from age 6, he was sexually molested by adult men. Police said they considered his account plausible based on details Bonacci provided. As Bonacci spent more time in county jail, he began telling stories of sexual abuse of minors by some prominent men in Omaha ... In a report accompanying the indictments, the grand jury [said] ... "He has been diagnosed as having multiple personalities, and his psychiatrist doubts that he can tell the truth.

His many inconsistencies and contradictions render his testimony unbelievable and necessitate his indictment for perjury."

Two Lawyers Put Owen Case to Jury Defense: She's a Sexual Victim Who Challenged the Powerful, June 19, 1991, *Omaha World-Herald* (p. 17): Alisha Owen is on trial because she dares to accuse powerful people of sexually abusing minors, then refused to back off from her allegations, her attorney said Tuesday. In his closing argument, defense lawyer Henry Rosenthal Jr. said the FBI had tried unsuccessfully to persuade Miss Owen to recant her allegations of sexual abuse. ... "She's sitting in that chair because she had the audacity to name Wadman [former Omaha police chief] and Andersen [Harold W. Andersen is the retired *World-Herald* publisher]."

Judge Dismisses Perjury Charges Against Bonacci, June 22, 1991, *Omaha World-Herald* (p. 11): All three perjury charges against Paul Bonacci were dismissed Friday within hours of the conviction of Alisha Owen.

The Franklin matter would have ended up under the carpet and all the other victims forgotten if it hadn't been for Gary Caradori, an ambitious investigator hired by the legislature after the two grand juries met, who continued seeking the truth about what really went on in Omaha. He contributed to John DeCamp's civil suit of Paul Bonacci versus the Catholic Archbishop of Omaha and Lawrence E. King, Peter Citron, Alan Baer, Harold Andersen, and other Nebraska persons and institutions.

Caradori went over thousands of reports of child abuse and trod further into the lion's den in order to discover what else lay behind the mess that Omaha was eager to forget. (Many of these complaints are documented in the film *Conspiracy of Silence* and are an element that added to the satanic panic in Omaha.)

But his investigation ended when his private plane was observed by one eyewitness to disintegrate in the air over

Illinois on July 9, 1990, with him at the wheel and his young son aboard. Robert Wadman's new jurisdiction was in Aurora, Illinois, and he was on the scene quickly. No one bothered to raise the concern that Wadman was one of the very men Caradori was investigating. All evidence concerning the aircraft disaster was destroyed, and DeCamp's investigation was dropped.

GARY CARADORI

Chronology of Events Linked to Franklin Credit Union, July 25, 1990, *Omaha World-Herald* (p. 14): July 11, 1990: A small plane piloted by legislative committee investigator Gary Caradori and carrying his 8-year-old son Andrew crashed about 2:30 a.m. into a north-central Illinois cornfield, killing both. Caradori and his son had attended the Baseball All-Star game in Chicago and were flying back to Lincoln [Neb.]. July 12, 1990: Some persons in Nebraska, including some members of the Caradori family and Franklin Committee Chairman Loran Schmit, raised the possibility that the Caradori plane might have been sabotaged because of Caradori's work for the Franklin committee. But chief federal investigator William Bruce, Lee County Sheriff Tim Bivins and County Coroner Richard Schilling said they hadn't seen any evidence of sabotage.

Safety Board Finds No Sabotage in Caradori Crash, July 9, 1992, *Omaha World-Herald* (p. 17): Three days before the second anniversary of Gary Caradori's death, the federal agency that investigated the airplane crash that killed the Franklin legislative committee investigator listed several possible causes. Not listed as a possible cause: sabotage of the aircraft.

Years later, I listened to Alan Baer brag at a church Christmas party how he had avoided the ax by simply pulling all of his foundation money out of Omaha for a year. His money, along with the Brandeis fortune, influenced and pretty much controlled many facets of the city, so no one had gone after him, thus solidifying his power. Able to buy his way out of anything, the man was basically his own state and could walk away entirely free from any fallout.

After David's death, I felt that never seeing Alan's monkey face again would be a blessing. When Caradori's plane went down, I knew Alan had won and there was nothing that could be done about it. What I didn't know was that he had plans concerning me. Because he was heavily connected to the people from my past, I now know that is why Alan Baer refused to leave me alone.

Years later, I would return to Omaha, and he and I would become involved in one last dance.

9

TRAVELS IN THE DESERT

One major consequence of being a ritually abused child is that traumatic memories are generally blocked out most of the time, and can even stay blocked forever. A similar thing happens to soldiers when they come away from a war in which they witnessed unspeakable things. If lucky, they may forget completely, but many get PTSD. Nightmares or "daymares" pop up (sometimes called flashbacks) and give the soldier almost an exact re-enactment of what he or she went through. Flashbacks can occur immediately or years later.

I did not accept that what I was experiencing were flashbacks of abuse until 2000, after my mother died, and I did not begin to put together my family's involvement until a few years ago, after my father's death.

The only way I can describe my perspective at this time of my life is that even though I knew so much, I avoided dwelling on it to the point where I wasn't able to see the bigger picture happening around me. "Remember to forget" was a mantra that I was taught as a child, and I did everything possible to do just that. The truth of the matter was that I wasn't ready or able to admit the truth of what had happened, so I just blundered on blindly, emotionally paralyzed and in the dark.

It was the injustice that occurred that was the hardest to take. For reasons I was unable to articulate, I was so fractured that I had no hope of repair and thus became desperate to get away from Omaha, my family, and most of all from myself. Beaten in a way that most people never have to go through, I suffered a great sense of defeat over what was finally seeping through to me and that was this: the people responsible for stealing my childhood were somehow responsible for hijacking my young adulthood as well.

So I bought a one-way ticket and with $60 in my pocket headed toward BJ. I'd forgiven him, knowing that he had been caught in Alan Baer's crosshairs. He was living with his mother and her boyfriend, Jeff, and I had no idea what I was walking into.

After a month with him in Massachusetts, I realized he was a bigger mess than I was, so I ended up sending him back to his grandparents in Omaha with the money we'd set aside for an apartment. In the process, I became homeless. He was undergoing a breakdown and was suicidal, and as cold as it sounds, I had no interest in trying to help him.

I was estranged from my family, even from my mother. Although she had saved me by sending me to Florida, she was still involved in Omaha and the events of my childhood in ways I didn't yet understand. I had grown uncomfortable with her, and considering what had just transpired, I didn't know who to trust anymore. The only thing I knew for sure was that I couldn't trust BJ, even though I did my best to try.

Fortunately, BJ's mom and Jeff had broken up, so Jeff offered to let me stay with him in Nashua, New Hampshire, and work at his mailing company out of his garage. I accepted gratefully, and it turned out to be the longest job I've ever had—and the most stressful.

Jeff, a decent man, was incredibly demanding. As an only child, he was used to getting his way and prone to temper tantrums when he didn't. In his early forties, he was a successful businessman who fashioned himself as somewhat of a playboy, womanizing every chance he could.

Despite the fact that Jeff was hedonistic and temperamental, I grew quite fond of him. He had a great sense of humor and was one of the most generous people I'd ever met. I found him endearing in a way that was refreshing, the best part being that he was safe and in no way connected to Omaha and my past.

Despite my attempts to suppress the past, I often found myself overwhelmed, and depression would put me in bed for days. I couldn't eat and all I had the energy to do was sleep and pee. I avoided human contact and personal hygiene for days at a time, unable to talk to anyone about what was bothering me. Sleep was the only way to prevent it all from constantly replaying in my brain.

Unable to cope with my depressions, Jeff eventually gave me a month to find another job and place to live. He promised to help me in any way he could as I quietly accepted his decision and made plans to go.

I'd be homeless the next year and a half as I drifted from one place to the next. I made friends with people willing to put me up and stayed until my welcome wore out, which it always did. I was fired from every job I found, generally because I was a complete and utter screw-up. Waiter jobs were a dime a dozen, so I went from place to place, working a couple of months at a time before being terminated, living hand to mouth in Boston, going from one gay guy to the next.

In fact, I started sexually acting out, often not even knowing my sex partner's name. Believing I was fated to suffer, I made the decision to begin exploring the life I'd denied myself. I figured if I was going to burn in hell, I might as well enjoy myself. Becoming promiscuous was breaking all the rules but was liberating at the same time, and anonymous sex provided a wonderful escape. Discovering that men actually wanted me empowered me, and sex was the only power I felt in my life. I started to become addicted to the experiences.

The emptiness of the superficial gay lifestyle is undeniable. When the meat market bars closed and the music, lights, and glitter disappeared, I'd either go home with someone or not. Everyone was looking for someone, be it a lover or a one-night stand, so while it was easy, it was also very lonely and almost impossible to make friends.

Growing up gay in America is far from a picnic, and many gays are often severely jaded by the time they reach adulthood. Effeminate males, having it the worst, are often singled out while growing up; so many gay men are filled with stories of abuse, either at the hands of their family or bullies in school. Not to say every homosexual is a product of abuse, but I have found that there is an undeniable constant there.

Homeless much of the time, I slept on the couches and floors of friends who let me live with them. Until you're actually homeless, it's hard to imagine the *soul exhaustion* of not having a secure place to lay your head. What I remember most was not having keys, a symbol of security. No place to live, no car, an armful of clothes, and no keys.

No longer able to feed myself and starving as a result, I decided out of the blue to call my father and ask for his help. The first and only time he ever helped me, to this day I still don't understand why he did it. He bought me a one-way ticket back to Omaha so I could return to my mother's apartment. I thanked him profusely, packed what little clothes I had left, and headed back to Wonderland.

Thirty minutes from Omaha, despite the fact that I was on a plane full of strangers, it all overcame me and I began to openly sob about returning to a hell I believed I would never again escape. Grief and fear crashed over me in waves and although it was a relief to finally have a stable place to live, returning to Omaha was another defeat on my long list of indignities, and I hated being back. Little did I know at the time but I was actually on the road to my salvation!

THE ONLY CONSTANT IS CHANGE

The early 1990s gay lifestyle was night and day from what it was in the mid-1980s. Stars and The Hollywood were gone, The Stage Door had wound down and closed, and The Max now dominated the bar scene. The Run had been cleaned up and police were patrolling the area, arresting both trade and their johns alike. After-hours was still going, but The Run was no longer the teenage hangout it once was.

Alan Baer had faded into the background and was no longer the party animal he'd been—at least as far as the gay community was concerned. Larry King was in jail. My mother's friend Peter Citron, with whom she worked at the *Sun* newspaper until it

Peter Citron[III]: David's mother

closed, was either dead or dying of AIDS in prison, and the "famous three" had been silenced.

PETER CITRON

Ex-WH writer Peter Citron Dies, June 28, 2003, *Omaha World-Herald* (p. 4b): Former entertainment reporter Peter Citron ... has died. Citron, 63, had been a *World-Herald* columnist and reporter for WOWT-TV. He was found dead Thursday in his home on Happy Hollow Boulevard ... appeared he had been dead for at least two days. ... an autopsy indicated Citron died of natural causes, but the exact cause may never be known. [Nine paragraphs later] ... In February 1990, he was charged with two counts of felony sexual assault of a child—accused of fondling two young boys in separate incidents. He resigned from the *World-Herald* and was convicted in May 1990. Citron was sentenced to three to eight years in prison and was paroled in January 1993.

Kevin Dobson

Other than Contra supplier Gilberto Montoya appealing for a new trial in 1991 regarding the drug connection with Kevin Dobson, his pot dealer friend Mike Dillon, and Garcia-Escobar—all Contra suppliers themselves—there was little evidence that there had even been a cocaine problem in the Omaha area. Working with the CIA, Kevin had helped bring down Pablo Escobar's drug cartel in the Contras and was in turn rewarded with obvious immunity and protection, considering he never went back to prison and is still living today.

With all the loose ends neatly tied up, Omaha had been tamed and had seemingly returned to normal.

Everyone I'd known had scattered, except for BJ, now divorced and living with a friend of ours and her five kids in Omaha. My mother's drinking had increased, and she was back to living with the man who had raped her years before when she lay in a diabetic coma. Resembling Bill Paxton in *Weird Science* when he turned into a drunken, pus-spouting creature, my mother's roommate had sores all over his body from not bathing, and the smell of decay always wafted around him, often making me want to retch.

Basically pretending that past events hadn't happened, we just went on with our lives, busying ourselves with everyday living while doing our best to avoid the elephant in the living room and the fact that this guy had raped my mother. I moved out as quickly as I could, but I still lived near my mom so I could keep a closer eye on her.

My father and stepmother, with the two children she had produced in 1975 and 1985, had moved back from Iowa and were living in West Omaha, in an upper-middle-class suburb. Dad may have helped me get back to Omaha, but we remained estranged, given that I couldn't stand him or my stepmother. Living some distance apart, with him in the nice part of town and me in the ghetto, we never ran into each other.

My sister Sarah had also moved back from Minnesota with her husband and four children, and although she lived a mere ten minutes from my father's house, she remained estranged from him as well. She and her family occasionally came to visit Mom, so I began to develop a relationship with her very different from when I was a child and we were subject to our parents' divide-and-conquer mentality.

Neither I nor any of my siblings have ever been close or trusting of each other. Cindy and Stephen had a somewhat close but tumultuous relationship, but Sarah had grown up like me, isolated and despised, as each of us was compelled to set the other up for our father's amusement and to win his acceptance. Of all my siblings, I was closest to Cindy.

Our brother Stephen was also living in Omaha with his new wife. While I was on the East Coast, he'd returned to Omaha with his family to mooch off my mother until, immediately upon my return, I threw him and his family out. It would stand as the last time we ever spoke to each other. I always did my best to avoid my siblings, as it was common for the police to have to get involved in our family gatherings. Stephen and his wife shared the same alcoholism as my mother and my sister Cindy's kids, and one could never predict what would happen in their company. Addiction ran rampant in my family, chaos was always right in tow, and I found it best to avoid rather than engage in the pandemonium.

I began attending the Metropolitan Community Church in town where I met a local school teacher named Art. A decade older than I, Art was also a fundamentalist Christian who would become instrumental in helping to set me on the path to my return to God. We often disagreed about religion and God, but he was like no other Christian I'd ever met in that he lived by example and treated others how he wanted to be treated, believing that love conquered all.

Always a gentleman, he never once made a pass at me, and I came to enjoy his company more and more. I was working job after job and living in place after place, so in a way Art was my only stability. I was no longer shoplifting, doing drugs, or hanging with bad crowds, but I was still a lost soul.

In fact, I was sexually active in a way I hadn't been before and was quickly succeeding in making a name for myself as the town whore. I went dancing alone every weekend at The Max, but rarely left that way. Art tried to impress upon me the consequences of my behavior, but at that time I wanted to be desired and found solace in the company of strangers. Feeling that my body was the only thing I had going for me, I had decided to travel down the path of debauchery—single, free, and loving every minute of it, or at least that's what I told myself.

Feeling as if I had no one to love and no one left to love me, I often chose to simply stay home—alone. Unable to keep any kind of job, there were days that I couldn't get up, let alone get out my door. It wasn't exactly agoraphobia, but part of me was scared of becoming overwhelmed in public, given that Omaha was a huge vat of bad memories for me, and everywhere I went pulled at my heartstrings.

As a result, I spent a great deal of time reading books, writing in my journals, and indulging in nostalgia, reminiscing over the adventures David, BJ, and I had when we first got together.

Hanging out with Art and listening to what he had to say about how I was living my life made me realize how incredibly lonely I was. Lying in bed one night unable to sleep, I asked God to either send me a dog or a boyfriend. A day and a half later, Sira entered my life.

A couple of guys walking in the neighborhood had thrown a German Shepherd/Golden Lab mix puppy over the fence where BJ's girlfriend's children were playing, never returning. BJ encouraged me to come and take a look at their new dog, but recognizing her in the same way I had David, I claimed her as my own.

After the weekend, after no one claimed her, I decided I was meant to keep her, considering her a gift from God. Naming her Sira, the female form of Sirius, I was unaware that hers would be the first relationship I would be given that was safe and sound and, most importantly, one in which I was needed! Just a dog, Sira would teach me more than I could have ever guessed about myself.

I found work as a banquet waiter, a job that I actually kept for some time, but although the pay was good, the hours were intense and the work laborious, and I often came home tired and stressed. Knowing that Sira was waiting for me was a comfort, and it was the thought of losing her that often forced me out of bed and off to work in the mornings.

As my constant loving companion, she offered me a relationship that would continue to heal me until she died of old age, when I was in my thirties.

God often speaks in strange ways. Sira may have been only a dog, but she was the first being to teach me about unconditional love. A gift from the Universe, she helped me to realize that God wasn't finished with me, while helping to renew my faith as a living example of an answered prayer.

MARCHING GAILY FORWARD

Sex, like most things in my life, has always been, for me, rather weird. As the product of ritualized sexual abuse, I often found myself disconnected and conflicted about my sexuality.

Although I viewed the sexual act itself as dark and somewhat dirty, I was still addicted to the physical contact I was getting from my anonymous encounters as well as the power in being desired. In the process, I was making a bad name for myself in town and reinforcing my negative perception of myself.

Feeling powerless in every other aspect of my life, I felt compelled to sleep with as many men as I could and being a top in a city of bottoms, it was easy to get laid. Let's just say if I had been able to afford a bedpost, it would have been filled with notches, and leave it at that. If the gay lifestyle is known for anything, it is sex, and I had every intention of taking advantage of that fact.

Driven by loneliness and sexual compulsion, I hung out in bars on weekends and parks and bookstores the rest of the week. This behavior can be typical of sexual abuse survivors, but it was hard to say what was truly behind my many sexual encounters.

BJ had returned to the East Coast to live with his mother, once again leaving his life in Omaha behind him, which included me. We were still pseudo friends, but had drifted apart, unable to speak about the very things necessary. My mother was drinking constantly, so apart from Sira, I had very few people to hang out with.

Omaha, for the most part, has always been "closeted." For example, both Larry King and Alan Baer were married, yet their propensity for young men was well known. Omaha parks were filled with homosexuals who were married, confused, and scared. These were men who found solace in the company of gay men. With The Run closed down, there was nowhere else to hang out or hook up. Many times, guys just wanted to talk, so I spent hours listening and talking about what it was like to be young and openly gay with men who, even if for a moment, enjoyed life through my eyes. Coming to relish my new capacity, I believed that for the first time ever I was actually helping people.

I was always between jobs, unable to endure the stress of being out in the public all the time, thus I had little social contact, considering most people usually get all the contact they need at work. Anonymous sex was a great escape for me, as often the sex was merely incidental; the real attraction was the company, which I used as an escape from living constantly in the memories in my head.

Years later in therapy, I would learn that what I was doing was called *displacement*, escaping my emotions by projecting them onto something or someone else so that I didn't have to face them.

Promiscuity, however, takes a toll on the soul, and it's hard to respect yourself when people are whispering about what a whore you are. The gay community in Omaha has always been small, but after the Franklin thing it had become even smaller, and gossip is often harsh.

Full of single prima donnas, the focus in Omaha's gay community had gone from the continual party back to the traditional lifestyle values of worshipping youth, beauty, and sex; and everybody was in competition with everyone else for every good looking man who happened to be in the bar at that moment. I told myself that the gossips were just jealous and that who I slept with was my business, although I couldn't count, let alone tell you, the names of the sexual encounters I had back then.

No longer into drugs and never much of a drinker, I spent weekends dancing on the speakers at The Max, four-foot-high platforms raised over the dance floor, where I could dance and watch the people down on the floor. The darkness that had once dominated the gay scene in Omaha was gone, and dancing on the speakers at The Max was sometimes the only safe place I had to go. Enveloped in my own little world, I would concentrate on the beat of the music, visualizing the energy that was all around me, using my intense weekend workouts for manifestation, prayer, and giving thanks for whatever I was thankful for.

While I was out searching for sex, I pretended God didn't exist. Out of sight, out of mind, afterward I'd make excuses explaining away my behavior, and since there was no real attachment to anyone, I found the lack of real intimacy safe. Primarily based on my background and the defenses I'd developed in order to survive, I had concluded that sex was power, and I needed whatever power I could muster.

Semi-dating several men at the same time became customary, which was social suicide in the bar scene. BJ's saying, "If they aren't paying my bills, feeding my face, or sucking my dick, I really don't care what people think," became my mantra, and I dismissed the effects my behavior was having on me.

THE WONDER OF LOVE

A little over a year after Sira came into my life, I was a carefree bachelor and loving every minute of it, or at least that's what I told myself every morning I woke up alone. Even though I was fucking a lot of guys, I never allowed them to sleep over, and when I stayed at their place, I left right after sex. To avoid any chance of a relationship forming, I tried to date unavailable guys who were either married or had a boyfriend. Married guys were preferable because they generally want only sex.

I tended to avoid parties, but one night I'd promised a friend that I would go to a party a mutual acquaintance of ours was throwing, figuring it wouldn't end up in an orgy like many after-bar parties did. The freedom that comes with being gay can be taken to extremes, usually by young "twinks," and it was hard to know if you were going to hang out or whether it would end in a free-for-all.

Being a one-on-one kind of guy, I was panicked by the group thing, so I'd usually leave at that point. Within walking distance from my apartment, I figured that if anything got jiggy, I would just excuse myself and slip out. However, as I expected, the party turned out to be quite tame, with people hanging out, drinking beer, and talking.

I scanned the crowd to see if I knew anyone. And that was the first time I would lay eyes on Tristan. There was something about him that I instantly recognized, though I had no idea what it was or who he was. In his early twenties, his looks were nice: blond, 5 feet 8 and cute. But there was something else, something deeper.

Although we stayed in our respective groups, we both caught each other staring at each other, and I couldn't stop thinking that I was going to end up spending the rest of my life with him.

When the party came to a close, I positioned myself in such a way that he had to walk past me. With a big smile, he said hello and asked if I would walk him to his car. Introducing himself, he explained that he was starting a new job and was new in town, knowing no one but his roommates, and barely at that. We were mesmerized with each other, so we made plans to go to the zoo later that week, which in Omaha is quite spectacular; we exchanged phone numbers and said good night.

Just out of college, Tristan was a new assistant manager at a local music store, struggling to make his way up the retail corporate ladder. He'd never been in a real gay relationship and explained that he didn't want to rush into anything. I emphatically agreed with him, telling him that I was just interested in friendship and nothing more, although I couldn't get past the feeling that I'd known Tristan before, like in another life, as everything about him seemed familiar.

At the end of our first night out together, he offered to drive me home. As we pulled up to my place, I told him that if he wanted to spend the night, he had to park around the corner, which he did immediately. Not exactly sure what the hell I was doing, I led him upstairs and we had a night of incredibly passionate sex. I allowed him to spend the night, and from that moment to today (eighteen-plus years at this point), he has never left.

It definitely wasn't all roses and champagne. We often had terrible fights that would end in vicious screaming matches. In fact, the first fight occurred the night he officially moved in. I immediately took out to the trash the Ouija board he'd just recently purchased, declaring I wasn't going to have that crap in my house because you never knew what doors flew open while playing with it. He was yelling that I was being superstitious and unreasonable, not having a clue as to my past, but I was not to be swayed, and I was accustomed to getting my way.

It was as if we couldn't get enough of each other. Spending every waking moment we possibly could together, we got to know the intricacies of each other's personalities quickly. The more I discovered about Tristan, the more I loved him. His work ethic was like none I had ever seen, given that he'd worked a job since he was fourteen. Giving, compassionate, and funny, he usually makes friends and rarely enemies, opposite to my experiences.

Exactly what he saw in me, I couldn't say, but the fact that I could see in his eyes how much he adored me every time he looked at me became intoxicating and I couldn't get enough of him.

Outside pressure arrived eight months into our relationship. My mother developed pancreatitis due to her alcoholism and, though surviving death once more, her kidneys permanently stopped functioning in the process. No longer able to care for herself, she had to choose between living with one of her adult children or going to a nursing home.

I impressed upon Tristan the thought that if he loved me, then he was going to love my mother, assuring him that she should come live with us. At no time did he offer an argument, seeking only to please me, so we began planning for her, unaware that we'd begun a miraculous journey. A month later, the five of us (including Sira and my mother's cat) began living together with no clue as to how we were going to do it. We just rolled up our sleeves and got busy with the day-to-day process of getting along.

Like everyone else, my mother took to Tristan immediately and became a surrogate for the mother he'd lost when he declared his homosexuality. Only seeing her drunk once, and briefly at that, Tristan had no exposure to my mother's alcoholism, but having the same issues in his childhood, he understood her in ways that I was yet unable.

Forbidden to drink in our house, mom spent her last five and a half years sober and on dialysis three times a week. We took care of her, not foreseeing that it would solidify our relationship in a way that nothing else could have. Everything happens for a reason, and this was no different. What we didn't know was that a family explosion was brewing and that my family's past was once again getting ready to rear its ugly head.

10

THE DRAGON STIRS

round the time my sister Sarah turned forty, she had a nervous breakdown triggered by memories from the past. When she began talking about events everyone else wanted to stay buried, she broke the family silence in a way that none of us could have seen coming. This was in late 1994 to early 1995.

My father had been trying to reach out to the four of us for some time, first to Cindy and Stephen and eventually to Sarah and me. Considering the years of next to nothing but bad memories, I still desired a father at the same time, so I reached out, desperate to have a relationship with him, though expecting the worst. Regardless of the events of the past, I loved my father and blamed my wicked stepmother solely for much of the abuse I suffered in their household. I did what I was taught and compartmentalized the past.

So, for all intents and purposes, the four of us were all in contact with him when Sarah began dredging up the past and talking about it. For years, we four had been at each other's throats, setting each other up, sacrificing each other in order to survive while listening to our father criticize everyone in my family as if he and his third family were some sort of prize. His divide-and-conquer strategy demanded silence or suffering the consequences of making waves, so we set up each other to take the hits, deflecting his disapproval, thus earning a reprieve as his "chosen one."

It was a game no one could win for very long, and it succeeded in driving us apart.

Accustomed to being the ugly duckling that everyone picked on, Sarah finally earned our father's good graces for the first time in her life when she began attending college to obtain a degree in social work in order to become a therapist. Proud that one among his offspring was actually going to college and getting a degree, my father constantly impressed upon us how Sarah was making something of her life and the rest of us weren't. Cindy and Stephen refused to praise my sister for her hard work, instead waiting for her to make a mistake so they could pounce on her and knock her from her pedestal.

They didn't have to wait long. Plagued with nightmares and childhood memories she had repressed for years, Sarah began losing sleep. Combined with the stress of raising a family, going to school, and being unable to come to terms with what she was remembering, she began speaking about her abuse for the first time, and she created a ripple that soon became a tidal wave that inundated the entire family.

Recalling Hummel Park, a city park on the northern outskirts of Omaha where many of the satanic rituals took place, she began to speak about our father's practices as high priest and the human sacrifices and terrible abuse that took place at the hands of both our parents and their friends. She obsessed over the past, unable to escape the memories flooding in, while she constantly talked about our past abuse, I guess to tried to process what had happened.

Cindy and Stephen conspired to tell Dad what Sarah was saying in order to destroy her budding relationship with him. A few minutes before Sarah was to visit our father, my brother called and told him what Sarah had been saying. Dad confronted Sarah and her husband at his front door and asked if there was truth in what my brother had just told him. Probably figuring that there was nothing to lose at this point, Sarah simply looked him in the face and told him that she was finally breaking the silence.

As this was happening in the living room, my stepmother was on the phone with Cindy in Florida insisting she wasn't married to our father at that time (although she most definitely was), trying to use her claims to shield herself from Sarah's accusations.

Growing pale and repeating over and over that he was the "best father he knew how to be," our father finally asked Sarah and her husband to leave, saying he never wanted to talk to her again. He shut and locked the door almost symbolically as they left. He subsequently declared Sarah disinherited and that we were never to mention her name again, or risk suffering the same fate.

I later heard different versions of the event from Cindy, Sarah, and my father, similar in that they all saw themselves as the victim, and they were all angry and defensive. Left to rage with an intense anger that the past was coming up again, I had naively felt that it was all over and, believing our satanic history was better left in the past, was livid with Sarah for not keeping her mouth shut.

Cindy campaigned to convince me that Sarah was a crazy liar while at the same time offering details about our father wearing the red robes symbolizing blood sacrifice. Neither my estranged brother nor I bothered talking, as he was a constant mess, becoming a strange combination of all that was bad about our parents.

Our father defended himself by saying he wasn't perfect but had been the best dad he knew how to be, half-heartedly calling Sarah a liar, although on one level or another we all knew the truth. I couldn't admit to myself that our parents were responsible and that I should be blaming them so, instead, I focused my rage on Sarah and catered to my parents.

The whistleblower position is never easy. In many ways, everyone abandoned Sarah. No one believed the bizarre Devil-worshipping stories she told about our childhood, and everyone pretty much considered her a crazy liar, dismissing her memories as mentally ill fantasies. Needless to say, both my father and mother avoided talking about it, and we all did our best to forget Sarah, telling each other that she had always been a "trouble maker."

Once, while Sarah was visiting us, I asked my mother if she had sacrificed any babies in Hummel Park lately—my poor attempt to camouflage the situation with humor. A fight ensued. Sarah declared she had no interest in listening to our mother's denials. She called me a coward as she slammed the door behind her.

Doing what we always did, like many dysfunctional families do, we didn't speak for months. Along her journey she had to be hospitalized a few times, emotionally crippled by the injustices of our past. Now forced to deal with our childhood alone, Sarah found herself disbelieved by everyone, and shunned.

MOTHER DEAREST

Tristan and I rented a sunny house with light in every room and moved my mother into the brightest room. Complaining at first, she grew to enjoy the sunshine and looked out the windows when there was nothing on television. Surrounded by our friends, her social workers and visiting nurses, she began to enjoy company *without* Gordon's gin—chilled, no ice.

She would sit in the kitchen smoking cigarettes and tell stories about her youth, still able to bewitch a room with tales of her family during the Great Depression and her father, a renowned artist, who had helped support nine families when times were the roughest. He had worked as a graphic designer for Coca Cola years ago, she explained, and he had created some of the famous female caricatures associated with the drink. It was often hard to get a word in edgewise.

Now I see that my mother had not recovered from the reality of the past she *didn't* spin stories about. Once alcohol was disallowed and all her drinking buddies were either dead or off in bars someplace, she was left with just Tristan and me and a whole new lifestyle. Veering between being a loving, gracious individual to a version of the "Princess and the Pea" bitch accustomed to people doing her bidding, she found some old habits hard to break.

I was not willing to play the servant role although dialysis was a crapshoot. Sometimes handling it fine, other times she would come home sick and exhausted convinced that she was eventually going to die during her treatments, leaving us no choice but to attend to her needs.

Cantankerous and constantly exerting her independence, Mom spent a great deal of time hiring and firing home visiting aides and nurses, insisting that she hated being treated like she was deaf and stupid just because she was in a wheelchair. She'd quickly grow impatient until she lost patience with them, giving them an earful before ordering them out the door.

Even sick, she had presence, and people rarely questioned her when she was angry. Often telling her that I was going to wheel her down the hill and out into traffic, I learned to laugh off some of her over-the-top intensity when she aimed her frustration at me. I can thank Tristan for showing me how to do this, watching how he was always able to take things in stride.

Death was nothing new to me, however, given that almost every death I'd experienced in my traumatized life was a result of something horrible, so I did my best not to think of my mother's, despite the fact that she was wilting away before my eyes. I avoided contemplating death, finding it frightening and triggering at the same time.

Shamanism would eventually change my views, but the practice was still new to me while she was dying, and I didn't have the tools to adjust appropriately, trapped as I was in the caregiver syndrome in which I identified with her and her death while paralyzed by the guilt of not being able to do anything other than watch her wither away.

About eight months before she died, we brought in a hospice group. She argued adamantly against having hospice in the house, assuming we were giving up on her, but she finally conceded when I explained that her care was becoming too much for us to handle. It was hard to overlook the terror that was often in her eyes with regard to her impending death and how it made her struggle against her fate, sick as she was.

Hospice was extraordinary, and I came away with a great deal of respect for what I perceive to be the career's calling from God. Treating my mother with dignity and her decline with respect, they sought to make her comfortable in every way possible, while, at the same time, giving Tristan and me a much-needed break. They scheduled nurses, bath ladies, doctors, and social workers in such a way that enabled us to get away for greater periods and gave us time to focus on our relationship, as well as a chance to become involved with a gay friendly church that we had been introduced to.

A few months before my mother died, we were sitting at the table one morning when she looked up from her morning newspaper and said, "I want to thank you." Figuring that an insult was next from the queen of backhanded compliments, I braced myself and asked "why," not expecting to be shocked by her answer.

She looked me right in the eye and said, "This is the first time in my life where I have not been abused or able to abuse myself. I just want to be sure that you and Tristan know how grateful I am for giving me that opportunity."

At the time I was uncomfortable, and quickly changed the subject, although I will always consider that moment one of the fondest I have of my mom.

Unfortunately, I was unable to sleep for long periods of time due to the stress of taking care of my mother, which was what I figured was fueling my nightmares. Unknown to Tristan, I was still sleeping with men all over town, unable to control my sexual compulsions. Secrets are a killer in a relationship, and I spent much of my time enveloped in guilt, convinced I was a bad person and more like my womanizing father than I cared to admit.

Often in an emotional state of turmoil and flying off the handle over nothing, my guilt fueled my paranoia and I often accused Tristan of doing the same things I knew I was doing, provoking fights between the two of us. Both Tristan and my mom pushed me to fill out disability papers in hopes that I could get financial assistance for treatment. Both were convinced I desperately needed it. I was unable to keep a job, so Tristan started looking for employment that might support us both, and he encouraged me to get into therapy instead.

Crashing emotionally, I was acting out in ways I couldn't control. Certain that I would be unable to deal with my mother's death, I did anything I could to escape thinking about it. For a long time, I honestly hoped that I would contract a disease so I could die alongside her.

My siblings were pretty much out of the picture, given that they blamed my mother for what had happened in the past and wanted nothing to do with her. Tristan, coming out a year or so after we were together, had been dealing with the repercussions of telling his family that he was gay, so we basically found ourselves alone, except for our friends who came to visit us and Mom, when she was able to entertain.

In some ways the strongest woman I have ever known, my mother, for the most part, kept a positive disposition while demonstrating an undeniable grace throughout her decline. Our friends had no problem listening to her repeat her life stories, as her timing was impeccable and she was as captivating as Bette

Davis— smoking her cigarettes and pausing at all the right places to enhance what she was saying.

She could always make me laugh, and it was fun to watch her interact with others, although you could never predict what would come out of her mouth. Yet that was part of her charm: people either loved her or hated her. Those who loved her would go to the ends of the earth for her, and I grew to adore my mom in a way that I had never imagined possible when I was a child. She died at home with us.

A METAPHYSICAL CHURCH

In 1998, about a year before my mother died, I learned of an up-and-coming church in town that honored all paths to God, so we decided to check it out in hopes that it would offer us a well-deserved break and solace from my mother's overwhelming health crises.

This new church seemed more like a Las Vegas nightclub performance or pep rally for God than church, but the Sunday service was a celebration of music and messages of hope and love, and there were no songs about blood and no Eucharist, so at least it wasn't triggering.

The philosophy was simple. Through our actions, we create our own lives, and spiritual texts, with a touch of quantum physics, were used to explain divine energy. The Bible was considered a collection of stories that, if interpreted in a metaphysical manner, offered secret knowledge that we could then take within in order to bring ourselves closer to God.

Similar to what I had learned as a child, this church drew me like a moth to a flame. In a way, I believed that this new perspective on life would be liberating and thought perhaps that it held the answers I was desperately seeking. I was enamored with the message that I, with God's help, was master of my own destiny. Tristan and I not only started attending but sought to get involved in any way we could.

A week after the third denial of my application for disability for PTSD, I received a letter stating that the government now considered me disabled, and I started receiving a monthly disability check after a slew of government doctors finally decided I qualified.

The Internet had arrived and chat rooms were full of men looking for discreet sex so, while Tristan was at work, I'd begun disappearing at times, hooking up with men I met online, while neither Tristan nor my mother suspected. I excused my bad behavior by telling myself that I was unable to control myself, yet I couldn't deny that my compulsions had become a serious albatross around my neck, causing me to distance myself from those I loved in order to live a life of secrets. Just like my father.

My first round of therapy ended badly after I began seeing a psychiatrist who, unbeknownst to me, was known all over town as a drug pusher. The same doctor who was seeing Sarah, he gave me everything he was giving my sister, overmedicating me with pills that didn't relieve anything, probably because I was neither bipolar nor did I suffer from dissociative identity disorder (DID).

The 900 milligrams of Depacote he prescribed for me daily did nothing but make me fat, and, still unable to sleep, I was having worse and worse panic attacks. Hearing the talk around town about him, I realized he was a quack, but it was only when I was told that his nurse, who was also my therapist, had been talking about me to other patients, I quit everything. Spending the next couple of days sick in bed, I hadn't realized that quitting Depacote cold turkey can cause seizures.

I was overwhelmed at home and unable to contain my emotions enough to hold down a job. I signed up for courses at a university but couldn't concentrate on the material and dropped out. Because I needed something more than taking care of my mother and compulsive liaisons, I thought that volunteering at the church might help me focus my free time.

The leader of the church was a charismatic, larger-than-life kind of man named Sky St. John. Sky was an openly reformed alcoholic who was currently in a married relationship with his gay lover who worked in the church with him. A long-time lounge singer and performer, he had spent years in bars getting drunk and making money until he subsequently had an epiphany, after which he had gone to ministerial school, changed his name, and reinvented himself as a sort of metaphysical Southern Baptist tent–type revivalist.

Upon arriving in Omaha, he and his lover quickly took over a failing church, and their unorthodox efforts seemed to be paying off, drawing greater numbers of congregants each week.

Every Sunday morning, Sky would shine like a star on stage, pumping out pep talks about how we were all capable of dealing with the problems in our lives and how God loved us all and that the universe would provide for us if we could learn how to act in a way that helped manifest our prayers into reality.

This was the opposite side of the same coin with regard to my childhood, which is why I agreed with much of what was being said. Sky already had a following in town, filling more and more seats until it was standing room only, and though he impressed me as somewhat of a snake oil salesman, I still saw an opportunity in the church, figuring it couldn't hurt helping others to focus on God.

My old friend Art had always been in the background and assured me that God was the only way out of my predicament. He expressed extreme mistrust for the church we were attending. Seeing right away that Sky was nothing more than a con man, Art believed that Jesus was my only salvation and urged me to rethink my decision about getting involved with a church that believed in anything and everything.

After much discussion, we agreed to disagree and I kept going to the church, although in the end, I have to admit that Art was right.

Later, I would refer to Sky's flock as The Cult of Disillusioned, although Tristan aptly named it The Church of the Misfit Christmas Toys, in reference to the Rudolf the Red-Nosed Reindeer cartoon shown on television every Christmas. Nonetheless, the church would become a factor in our lives for some time to come.

Part of the draw for me was the community that I hungered for. Finally finding a place where we could be ourselves and still fit in, we began reaching out to what we felt was an extended family. The congregation was overflowing with eclectic individuals full of new although sometimes unusual ideas and convictions, and the church seemed like a place where everyone could share what they believed without judgment. Feeling as out of place in society as we did, many had gravitated to the church community for the same reasons, and in the beginning it was a very loving, giving place.

I volunteered to cook every Sunday morning for when service let out. Although it kept me out of the sanctuary when Sky was doing his thing, I loved the gratitude everyone expressed for the food.

Sky had big plans for his little church. He wanted to take it from a small congregation to a big radio-television *cult* ministry. Assuming control over everything, including the board of directors, Sky and his partner revamped everything while everyone eagerly jumped on board with few questions asked, excited by the prospects that Sky assured everyone were ahead.

Just weeks after our arrival, I began hearing rumors that Sky was sleeping with male members of the congregation. Figuring that a couple of fags running a church might inspire such rumors, I shrugged them off at first, because I was more interested in the community rather than its leadership anyway. Given time, however, I slowly began to realize it was a bigger issue than I thought when I began witnessing members drifting away or being run out.

No one seemed to notice or care, and like the Emperor with no clothes, Sky constantly surrounded himself with his devout fan base that did anything he asked. A dynamic speaker on Sunday mornings, he was no good when it came to the pastor-parishioner intimacy people crave, not to mention the fact that he was sleeping around all over town and everyone was gossiping about it.

Eventually, Sky and his partner held a divorce ceremony and publicly separated and, although at odds, continued running the church together.

Having been exposed to the gay lifestyle all my adult life, it wasn't the fact that Sky was gay that bothered me so much as his pretentiousness and the chaos that surrounded him. Tristan and

I were in a small although growing minority of church members. Then an incident furthered our growing rift.

Christmas has always been an especially bad time of year for me, as I could never help but to recall the past, and that year I had found myself overcome by the grief of what had been taken from me as a child regarding the sexual abuse I experienced. Triggered by one of my many trysts, it emotionally began to sink in how violated I have always felt, and the grief surrounding my objectification was devastating.

Not knowing what to suggest, Tristan urged me to go and talk to Sky, as he was our minister. Figuring what the hell, I called and made an appointment for us to go and see Sky at his home.

The meeting, needless to say, went badly. After listening to me for ten minutes, Sky declared, "I can help you overcome this drama by becoming your spiritual savior."

"I'm my own spiritual savior," I told him. "What I experienced was a little more than drama."

"That's because you're a drama queen," he retorted.

"You're not much of a savior," I said as Tristan pulled me out of the room.

On the walk home, I ranted at the top of my lungs, infuriated at being talked down to like I was a child. Tristan listened quietly, then demanded that I get a list of therapists from my mother's social workers and find a therapist as soon as possible.

A second incident occurred later between Sky and me at my mother's memorial service when Sky made a pass at my seventeen-year-old nephew, humiliating all of us. In the end, I would have very little goodwill left for the man, but the real *coup de grace* was when he went out of his way to bring Alan Baer back into my life, which became the proverbial last straw.

A TIME TO TALK

I had no one to really talk to other than Tristan and my mother, and I was keeping secrets from them, so you would think that I would have looked forward to seeing a therapist. But just the opposite was true.

Having no faith in therapy and basically attending the appointment I'd made to placate Tristan, Dr. Smith (obviously not her real name) had been last on the list of about fifteen therapists my mother's social worker had given me, but I liked something about her voice, so I left a message on her machine requesting an appointment.

Although my last therapist had been female, the nurse of that drug-pusher doctor, I still felt more comfortable talking with a woman than with a man. Honestly, straight men have always intimidated me. Not the ones I slept with (whom I never considered all that straight), but rather it is the butch, womanizing, beer-drinking man's man type that generally encapsulates the straight man persona that generally makes me nervous.

Neither overly feminine nor overly masculine, I still get paranoid by those who feel compelled to overexert their male sexuality. Of course, I could have chosen a gay therapist, but I couldn't see myself going to any male therapist, even a gay one.

Considering my background with the pedophilia perpetrated on me by Aquino, I am not surprised. He is probably the reason why I especially wouldn't see a gay male therapist. Not that I am suggesting that gay therapists are inherently bad therapists, but my experience had taught me not to trust many gay men due to their penchant for playing games with those closest to them.

Dr. Smith was attractive and professional. Fairly tall, smartly dressed, with styled hair and glasses, she looked like a competent therapist, although I knew I couldn't judge a book by its cover. Her small office was filled with psychotherapy books, a desk, a chair for her to sit on during our sessions, and a nice leather couch for clients. I felt comfortable almost immediately, so I decided to put everything on the table figuring she would respond like everyone else I'd told my story to.

I gave her a condensed version of my childhood. I offered the basics of my family background and how my older siblings and I had been destroyed by what we'd experienced, figuring she would dismiss me.

Prefacing it all by trying to explain that we are all products of our experiences, I told her about being taught to "see into people" in a way that often made them uncomfortable. Describing my relationship with God and the esoteric nature of my spiritual beliefs, I also told her of my fear of waking up and being the Antichrist. She listened intently and asked a few questions for clarification, and in this way we spent the first few sessions getting to know each other. Despite what I was telling her, she still wished to continue seeing me.

When she learned what church I was attending, she suggested that I pick up a book called *The Way of the Shaman* by Michael Harner as a way to approach my spiritual concerns. She commented that my "abilities" sounded shamanic in nature and thought that looking into a Native American way of spirituality might be a way to stave off my fears. Shamanism, she explained, primarily dealt with the practice of dream work. She suggested that it might be a way to help me master the nightmares that were so debilitating.

Declaring that it wasn't her job to confirm or deny my experiences but rather to help me to focus on learning to live everyday life and to face those things I was unwilling to face, she explained that therapy was useless if I wasn't willing to work hard at it. It could take years, she warned me. I was not to take therapy lightly, and I should commit the time to be in it for the long haul. Angry at first that she refused to take my side and wouldn't say whether or not she believed me or not, I have come to respect what she taught me throughout my years of therapy.

Everyone has defenses and mine were in full swing the first few months. I began to suffer from images of raping her in her office and as a result almost abandoned our work early on. Terrified of such fantasies, I told her that I no longer wanted to see her again, but after I explained why, she assured me that it was just my defenses at work to keep me from getting healthy, assuring me I would reach a point where I did not need them anymore.

It was a miraculous discovery to me when I learned to discern when my mind was fighting the therapy and how talking about it made the negative fantasies and defenses disappear. Designed to help me persevere during the horror of my childhood, the defenses that had saved me when I was young were now getting in the way of my having a productive and happy life as an adult, and the more I learned about myself, the more aware I became.

One example of one of my defenses was lying. Because I was uncomfortable around people, I learned to lie to safeguard myself by encouraging people to keep their distance. Originally, I lied to try and keep myself from being beaten while, at the same time, I used my lies to insulate myself from both the reality of the abuse and the humiliation I felt at being treated like an animal.

As a young adult, however, my old defense made for an incredibly lonely, self-isolating life. I would learn throughout therapy that once you realize a defense exists, you can change the behavior, but the key to this was gaining enough perspective to recognize the problem. Dr. Smith would spend years helping me face what I wouldn't face alone.

I learned a lot about post-traumatic stress disorder, and even reached a point where I could recognize when a panic attack was on the way. The attacks had always been bad, but lately had been getting worse. One even caused me to pass out in a department store. She helped me to become aware of the "triggers" that would begin the attack, which could be caused by an event, someone saying something in a certain way, or even smells.

Dr. Smith helped me with coping techniques. I even started becoming capable of identifying situations I didn't want to be in, as well as learning how to control the behavior that generally got me there. Assuring me that I was a normal person who had gone through some abnormal events, Dr. Smith often remarked that it was a miracle that I hadn't ended up as my dad had predicted, either dead or in jail, given that most people gravitate to what they know, and chaos and abuse was the norm during my formative years.

I have often been asked what I talk about in therapy and my reply is that I think of all the things I don't want to talk about and that's what I bring up in my sessions. Following the work of Carl Jung, Dr. Smith often concentrated on drawing out my shadow side, my darkness, so I could examine it. Throughout the years I have been with her, she has helped me bring my shadow into the light, thus, in a way, re-parenting me. She gave me the guidance and support I never received as a child.

At one point, my agoraphobia threatened our sessions. Often not wanting to leave the house or drive the car, I would cancel our appointments at the last minute, further hindering my treatment. It wasn't like Sigourney Weaver in the movie *Copycat* where she was paralyzed by the fear of her front door, but rather a case of my not wanting to feel exposed in public. Crowds stressed me, but not as much as driving, and many days the thought of getting out on the road was enough to make me stay in bed.

When Dr. Smith demanded that I honor my appointments or she would drop me as a patient—explaining that boundaries were exceedingly important to the therapeutic process and that she had a business to maintain—I began to discipline myself by forcing myself to attend therapy on a regular basis.

Most people see a therapist once or twice a month, but due to the abuse I had suffered and its uncontrollable effects, at one point I was seeing her three times a week. Given the amount of grounding, *de*programming, and *re*programming I needed, I have realized what a lifesaver Dr. Smith has been.

She helped me face the anger I felt toward my mother's drinking as well as the guilt I felt because of it by walking me through my emotions, Dr. Smith helped me to become a more complete person, sharing those tools necessary not only to identify and understand my thoughts and feelings, but also those that enabled me with the ability to articulate them as well.

I had spent a lifetime learning how to stay silent, and now being able to talk about the things that scared me the most helped lessen my fears and allowed me to understand myself more fully.

She explained the caregiver syndrome from which I was suffering, and she helped me focus on coming to terms with my mother's impending death while, at the same time, encouraging me to think of my future. Compassionate and patient, she didn't shy away from my intensity like most people did, and I respected her strength.

Finally, by pointing out how I was re-abusing myself every time I sought sexual gratification outside of love—an insight that had never dawned on me—she helped me to stop sexually acting out. Pointing out that my actions were not only hurting those around me, but myself as well, and in terrible ways, and thus she helped me face that the guilt I felt about sleeping around on Tristan.

I often remarked that I had no idea how to stop myself, but it wasn't until I heard it said out loud that I realized the truth was, regardless of what had happened to me in my past, I was still responsible for my choices as an adult, and my choices did indeed have consequences.

It is my contention that therapy is one of the greatest gifts you can give yourself. Finding a person who can help you truly examine what you really think and why, helping you to become more conscious of yourself, can be an invaluable asset.

Dr. Smith, however, was about to have her hands full, as my past was about to grab me by the balls once again. Wonderland was winding back up, only this time I wouldn't be running from the darkness, and what I would discover about myself would border on the miraculous.

SHAMANISM

My first real experience with Shamanism was with a woman named Cathy Burgess, a talented and gifted shaman in Omaha. A practicing nurse who had researched the subject thoroughly, she was an incredibly intelligent and gifted woman who eventually received a full scholarship to study for four years in Ireland and write about ancient Celtic shamanism.

Generally associated with Native American medicine men and women, shamanism is the first spiritual practice of humankind and is found in most cultures from Europe to Asia to Africa. Like the old *mythos-logos* paradigm, shamans perceive in a spirit world as well as our consensual reality; they know that *mythos* continuously plays out in our lives through guides, angels, demons, spirits, and ghosts.

By contacting the Kingdom of Heaven within, every individual has the capacity to interact with "the other side" through what I like to call active prayer. Instead of quieting the mind through meditation, the shamanic practitioner listens to a drumbeat in a darkened room with eyes closed and encourages the mind to go where it will. The participant experiences a waking dream in which the shaman receives guidance and information from guides on the other side, and this work is often symbolic and takes practice to master.

When I met Cathy, it was to seek her guidance in retrieving parts of my soul that I'd lost during the trauma and fear I'd undergone as a child. I lay on a blanket on the floor while she walked around me burning sage, blowing the smoke on me, while she shook a rattle, explaining that she was cleansing the area and asking for guidance and protection from her guides on the other side.

Though I felt uncomfortable and a bit silly, I also felt that I *had* lost parts of my soul. Scared and having no idea what to do while she went on her "journey," I closed my eyes and allowed my mind to wander as she lay down beside me, shoulder to shoulder, hip to hip, ankle to ankle.

To an onlooker, it would only have looked like two people lying together on the floor listening to the beat of a drum. Inside the mind is another matter altogether, as the drumbeat changes the brainwaves from beta to delta, tricking the mind into thinking it is asleep. In what is referred to as a waking dream, the shaman then can go anywhere he wants mentally through "astral projection" (be that geographically or forward or backward in time), all the while remaining in a dream state.

Not recognizing it at the time, I now understand how similar these beliefs were in comparison to what I was raised with and why I found the interest in it that I did.

I allowed my brain to wander while Cathy did her thing, and I suddenly saw myself in front of a small dark-haired woman who was walking toward me. I had no idea who it was, but I was taken at how well she could walk, although I had no idea why. She put her hand to my face and stroked my cheek, telling me how proud of me she was. Telling myself that I was only imagining this encounter, I was nonetheless in constant awareness of how upright she was moving, and with such agility.

Cathy completed her journey and sat me up. Cupping her hands on my head, she blew onto the crown of my head three times to symbolize the three aspects she had brought back from the upper world (a place that has little to do with the Christian sense of heaven), the lower world (which has nothing to do with hell), and the middle world, the world in which we exist. Relighting the sage and beating her drum, she walked around me singing and thanking her spirit guides for helping her and protecting us.

This ceremony, called a soul retrieval, enables the shaman to see a person for whom he or she really is, as well as aspects of their life they may be hiding, even from themselves. Finding the parts of the soul that have been lost throughout life, a Shaman is oftentimes given an overview of the person's life, and such was the case with Cathy, whose perspective regarding me had obviously changed.

With pure admiration in her eyes, she told me that she had never met anyone who had gone as far spiritually as I had, and she was convinced that I had an important role to perform here in this world. Not once giving her any details of my past or my belief that I was going to become the Antichrist, she was convinced regardless that I was some sort of gift from God and sent here to do something important.

Cathy's conviction that I was connected to God gave me hope that I might be able to thwart my fate as the Antichrist, and I decided to further explore what Shamanism might have to offer.

Power animals are guides found in the lower world who help guide and heal. Dependent on the shaman, these guides work on a very personal level, and I would later find myself doing quite a bit of work with the energies of Bear, Wolf, and Dragon, each of whom stood as symbols for attributes lending power to me. For example, when I feel weak or scared, I focus on Bear energy, bears being fearless, protective, and beautiful. I focus my mind on what it is to be a bear, and then try to emulate the feeling, visualizing the same attributes within myself.

When Cathy had set out to retrieve the parts of my soul I had lost in my first soul retrieval, Bear had immediately presented himself to her on the other side in order to help, and she assured me that this was significant in and of itself.

The day after my soul retrieval, I was talking on the phone with Cindy, detailing the event for her, but not until after she mentioned my dad's paternal grandmother who had died before I was born. The woman Cindy described made me immediately recall the woman I had "seen" during my soul retrieval the day before. She had been horribly crippled with osteoarthritis and could barely walk. It dawned on me that this could have been the reason why I was so impressed with how upright and agile my "apparition" was. I believed it was my great grandmother who had first greeted me from the other side, and it was the first time ever when someone in my family was actually proud of me.

Considering my past, it was easy for me to embrace Shamanism. In a way, Shamanism and Satanism are opposite sides of the same coin, which was exactly what worried Art. Both believe in God and the spirit world. Like satanic high priests, shamans deal with the spirit world and the archetypes within human psyches, but the primary focus is to create psychological and spiritual balance, not power—with nature providing an example of good balance.

Shamanism and Satanism both perceive the existence of psychic realms and the influence of angels and demons, though their interactions with these realms are as different as night and day.

Satanic power grows by taking energy from others, while shamans gain a sense of place by helping others heal. Both utilize rituals, although their practices are polar opposites. Instead of primarily focusing on daggers and blood, Shamans use drums and rattles. While satanists like to chant, Shamans like to sing, and though both use candles and incense to help focus the mind into helping the spirit commune with the other side of existence, satanists are much more aggressive than shamans, doing what they can to defile and separate themselves from the light; whereas, shamans honor the light and do what they can to live within it as planetary light bearers. Satanists prefer chaos, shamans balance. Satanists seek to derive power by invoking demons; shamans seek balance between light and dark, believing that both are *God experiencing God.*

Most different, however, is how shamans and satanists look upon death. Satanists achieve power by absorbing others' life force at their moment of death; whereas, shamans believe that true power is the ability to experience one's own personal death at will. By separating themselves from physical existence over and over again in shamanic practice, shamans learn to release the worries and bonds of life for the final separation. Learning how to move in and out of the energy of God and the universe improves one's "map" for when the time comes to achieve a truly worthy personal death.

Shamanism for me has been a gift. Most importantly, it gave me the ability and strength to explore the shadow side of my personality as well as the part of me that lives in the light. In comparison, I have found Shamanism's gentle and nurturing approach to be much more effective than the horrific experiences satanists subjected me to, believing they would strengthen me. Having the advantage of starting with a shaman-like belief structure early in life through the practice of Satanism, I have now garnered a much better understanding of the world in which I live and of myself.

Still, I would have to go head to head with the demons of my past and people would once again have to die.

11

THE SHOW COMES TO TOWN

S ky and The Cult of the Disillusioned began their campaign to become a power in the Omaha spiritual community, stepping up their efforts by moving into a school near the church while selling our current property in order to look for another more appropriate for the growing congregation.

Sky's sermons were attracting dozens of new people every Sunday, causing the church to growing exponentially, as well as the financial contributions. I became a "spirit singer," singing up on stage every Sunday morning to cheerlead for Sky at the beginning and end of every service. At that time, I still believed in the church, and my new exposure gave me the opportunity to get to know more of the congregation.

Sky introduced me to a woman named Susan and asked if I was interested in forming a fundraiser group for the upcoming land campaign. Susan headed the volunteer services at the church. Enthusiastically accepting, I thus began my relationship with Susan, a road that would lead to my downfall in the church.

Susan was both a practicing shaman as well as a Reiki master adept at manipulating energy, and I fashioned her as some kind of a fairy princess who was able to touch everyone with her magic personality.

Tristan and I developed a group called "Gifts from the Heart" and petitioned the congregation to offer their services, time, and money in a way that demonstrated their dedication to the land campaign. The plan worked splendidly, and we were able to garner over $90,000 in cash during the first eight months, as churchgoers couldn't seem to give enough for the new church.

The more involved we became, however, the more we heard about Sky, and many of the stories were quite disturbing. All smiles and light on stage every Sunday morning, Sky's dark side represented a perfect example of a nondrinking alcoholic or dry drunk. Although he was no longer getting drunk, his actions were that of a typical dry alcoholic—lying, lashing out, and blaming others—while he dismissed his bad behavior as mere eccentricities.

Common of many cult leaders, he surrounded himself with people who insulated him from many issues he needed to face. Members objecting to the direction the church was taking were being run out by Sky and his followers with tactics that isolated people until they felt they had no recourse but to leave.

Susan, hearing the same things we were, convinced us that dealing with people like Sky were a necessary evil when it came to building a church, and assured us that the good he was doing far outweighed the impact he was having on a select group who "probably couldn't be pleased anyway." Unconvinced, we nonetheless did our best to look past the problems, focusing on ourselves and what we were trying to do for the church.

Unconcerned with the effects he was having on people and unable to escape his narcissistic ego worship, Sky sought more

and more power making it only a matter of time before he attracted the attention of like-minded individuals like Alan Baer.

By this time, I had been befriended by one of Alan Baer's best friends (and the godfather of one of Alan's grandchildren), an ex-priest who had been involved with the founding of the Metropolitan Community Church in Omaha. Fred Zydek was the first of my "friends" to turn on me when I later began investigating my family.

Fred and his lover had come up to me after the service one morning and invited me to dinner. Explaining that they were breaking away from the Catholic Church, Fred and his lover had just newly joined the church and were looking for information on ways to become more involved. One of the beauties of The Cult of the Disillusioned was that you could be of any denomination, even a member of another church, and still become a member of The Cult of the Disillusioned, as it prided itself in celebrating all pathways to God.

In his late sixties, possibly early seventies, Fred stood at 6 feet 7 and weighed well over 300 pounds. Gregarious to the point of almost being overbearing, he was a complete opposite to his lover, who looked frail and often stood quietly in the shadow of Fred's personality. Often Fred would laugh, commenting that he was going to leave his lover for four fifteen-year-old boys, although they'd been together for more than thirty years.

Suspecting nothing sinister other than the fact that Fred had an appetite for young boys, I befriended the two men, disregarding their relationship to Alan Baer. Omaha was small, and the gay community even smaller, so encountering someone connected in some fashion to Alan wasn't all that unusual. I never considered the possibility that Fred was also somehow connected to the events of my childhood.

Both men were teachers by profession, and I enjoyed their intelligent conversation, as well as the fact that Fred often expressed dislike for Sky and his ex-lover, giving us something in common in discussing the gossip going around the church.

A couple of years ago, while reading *Ritual Abuse in the Twenty-first Century: Psychological, Forensic, Social, and Political Considerations* by Randy Noblitt and Pamela Perskin Noblitt, I learned that people associated with cults often seek out their childhood victims when those children become adults. The intent is to reestablish a connection with them in order to keep an eye on them. Standing where I do now, I realize that is exactly what Fred was doing, and it was no coincidence that he was intimately connected with Alan Baer.

Fred constantly encouraged me to let go of the past and forget about what happened when I was a child. Foolishly, I never once thought to consider why he would be so invested in how I dealt with my past.

The Devil never far away, my past was getting ready to come a calling again as Alan Baer was about to come back into my life for a third time, although this time his focus would be on Tristan.

FAMILY BOUNDARIES

No one in my family holds the truth in high regard, and finding history to be fluid, they can manipulate virtually any situation to fit the delusion or fiction of the day. Despite all of the dysfunction, however, having my sisters back in my life was a comfort. Whoever said that it's better to be alone than in bad company obviously had never been as lonely as I've been throughout my life.

Along with Sarah, I've always been the family scapegoat, especially for Cindy and her family in Florida. Never having come to terms with the damage done to her during her childhood she, as a result, had raised a family out of control. Embittered, she spent an inordinate amount of time creating misery for others.

On the other hand, I *did* believe her rumor that our dad was not the father of my stepmother's children but rather they were part of my *brother's* offspring. Inappropriate relationships abounding in our family, my stepmother was much closer in age to my brother than my father, and considering how touchy-feely she was with my brother, I found it impossible to rule out.

After my father and stepmother moved back to Omaha, Cindy began telling everyone that our stepmother had been molesting their young son in the shower. Talking with our father about it, I concluded my oldest sister was right and reported my parents to Child Protective Services (CPS). When I found out that Cindy had made a similar complaint to CPS three years before, I became enraged when, in order to protect our father, she called the local office and recanted, claiming that I was crazy and that the abuse wasn't true.

Sarah, a bigger family scapegoat than even I, was considered to be nothing but a crazy troublemaker whom both Cindy and our father tried to divide me against, although years later I would see through their bias, at which point we were able to compare notes about our childhoods.

As for my brother, he had become another version of my father—molesting his wife's children throughout their marriage. He never strayed far from his use of alcohol and needles and often found himself in trouble with local authorities. His ex-wife ended up on the national watch list of sexual predators, and my brother eventually died, in 2008, of hepatitis C, in Ocean City, Maryland. Years later, when I began to investigate my family, I discovered that he was more like our father than I had ever considered, intricately involved in our past in a way that I could never have suspected.

It was only a matter of time before the family gossip began flowing about me, but I dealt with the talk head on, even confronting my father about my physical abuse, figuring the only way to heal was to confront the issues head on.

Dr. Smith was concerned that I was once again in a detrimental relationship with my family simply for the sake of having them in my life. Once I learned that most of our behavior is unconscious, I committed myself to explore and articulate my intentions in order to try and avoid setting myself up by clinging to unreasonable expectations.

Growing stronger, I was beginning to accept what had happened to me and how I felt about it, which enabled me to write the following letter to my father the year after my mother died [shortened here]:

Dad,

It is Christmas and all day I have been thinking of you. In fact, I've been thinking about you for a lot longer than that, but today I finally picked up pen and paper to share with you my thoughts. Cindy told me recently that you were suffering from prostate cancer, so I figured I shouldn't waste any more time, as so much of it has already been wasted.

Many things have been coming together for me, mainly due to conversations between the two of us right before I concluded that

I needed to distance myself from you. Several issues have come up for me, things that have struck me as odd, and though I wasn't sure why at the time, I have reached a point of understanding that leaves no doubt in my mind.

Most of my life, I have blamed your third wife for the things that happened to me. Most of the abuse I can remember rotated around her, and I looked upon you as a weak and ineffective man who was too browbeaten to stand and defend his children. This began to change, however, after you and I got into the conversation regarding the time when you took me into the garage and beat me. You laughed when I said that you had beaten me with a 2x4, correcting me that it "wasn't a 2x4 but a 1x6, but it probably felt like a 2x4." Not realizing it at the time, I later realized that not only did you find humor in beating a 13-year-old child, but that you derived a sense of pride from it as well. Had the roles been reversed, and had it been me beating you, I seriously doubt humor would have been your response, and I found it incredibly painful and difficult to accept that my father could have such a callous disregard for my feelings regarding an event I found incredibly traumatic. Let me just say, before you begin defining my sense of trauma, anyone who gets beaten, regardless of the circumstances, experiences trauma. However, I did not recognize the full extent of the abuse, as you well know.

It was in one of our last conversations that I found the key to why I felt so strange telling you that it was neither natural nor right for a grown woman to be taking showers with an eight-year-old boy and having you respond that it was okay because she was making sure his back was clean. It is incomprehensible how a man could be willing to allow a child to be molested without feeling compelled to do something about it. Hearing you say this clarified for me that not only did you know what was happening, but you also condoned it. You found it acceptable that your wife was molesting your youngest son.

I am finally remembering what you did to me, dad. I remember you, your third wife, and me, all of us naked while I was forced to lie on your third wife while she held my butt so you could rape me. I don't need you to validate this for me, and I have had more than enough of your lies. It defines why I have had many of the problems I have with my life, why sex and intimacy are almost an impossible combination for me, and why I feel so alienated from the world, although I have a plethora of love in my life. The explanation is unfortunately simple: I had monsters for parents.

You know, dad, I can't even fathom what it must be like for the two of you to look in the mirror and realize that you are nothing more than a couple of perverted child rapists, monsters, who are not only capable of but guilty of incredibly sick sex crimes against children. Your very own children. . . .

What it must be like for you to know that you have created such pain in your life, that you are the kind of people other parents warn their children about. The hatred I feel for you at this moment is incredible. What you stole from me was something incredibly precious and sacred. Then to realize that you have gone out of your way to convince me that it was all my fault, that I was nothing more than a piece of shit who deserved everything I got. As you did with us all.

In writing this, I am finding it virtually impossible to remove the image of you reading this and becoming sexually aroused by the memories of what you have done, what you are probably still doing with your youngest child. I hate what you have done, I hate what you stand for, I hate who you are, and most of all, I hate *what you've done to me. I hate feeling so violated, and I am in incredible mourning for what you willingly, selfishly, and brutally took from me. From all of us.*

One of the hardest aspects of all of this for me, dad, is that even though I hate you beyond belief, I also love you. You are my father, and boys need their fathers. So knowing myself, I realize I will reach a point of forgiveness, although I am far from that now, and I find it heartbreakingly frustrating that you and I will not be able to work this through in order to heal. Obviously you and your third wife suffered severe abuse as children, but you had no right to inflict the same devastation on us. There just isn't enough time to heal from this. . . .

I am no longer going to protect your secrets, and there is no reason I should. I have no guarantee that you won't just continue with your youngest, and I feel compelled to honor my responsibility to protect children when I can, unlike you who use them to get off by raping them. . . .

You know I am telling the truth, and you know, given the opportunity, it will not be that hard to show that you both are child rapists. Although courts can't heal the wounds, exposure will bring out the truth. Your secrets have done nothing but serve you and hurt everyone else involved, and I for one have had enough. What I want is not validation, for I know what happened. Nor do I need you to say you believe me. What I want is vindication, and if there is anyone in this family who can accomplish that, it is me. . . . I think you've been hoping and praying I wouldn't remember because you knew that if I did remember what you had done, I wouldn't take it lightly and I certainly wouldn't take it lying down. You raped me, dad. I know this now without a shadow of a doubt, so stop trying to kid me or yourself. Physically, mentally, emotionally, and sexually, you have been nothing less than a monster.

Empowered by finally telling the truth, I sent the letter not only to my father but to all of my siblings, as well as taking it to my stepmother's church and their son's school. Although nothing came from any of it other than alienating me further from my father and stepmother, telling the truth was liberating for me, and I relished the feeling despite the fact that it caused so much chaos in the family.

I could never have foreseen the changes that my correspondence would have on my father, or, as we got the closer to his death, how important my letter would become to him in the end.

AND THE BAND PLAYED ON

Back at The Cult of the Disillusioned, Susan and I thought that a cookbook would be just the thing to bring the congregation closer together. It was at a chaotic time, due in part to the church's growing pains and pressures of fundraising for the building campaign, although money was pouring in from everywhere and Sky was filling the seats every Sunday.

A few months into the Gifts from the Heart fundraising project, Alan Baer's assistant Chris called our home (having gotten our number from Fred), in order to schedule a time for Alan to discuss with us the fundraising campaign and a financial contribution he was considering donating.

Suddenly, Alan jumped on the phone, and though neither of us referred to what had transpired years before, I agreed to meet with him, figuring that any contribution was good, regardless of who was making it. Never in a position to say no to the man, I was not happy about seeing him again.

How I could have anything to do with him after what had happened between us is not an easy issue for me. First, it was with good reason that I believed nothing could be done to stop the man. Skirting the Franklin Credit scandal, his power in Omaha was visibly incontestable. Never once held accountable for the crimes he was guilty of, other than paying a nominal fine for soliciting sex, he was untouchable until the day he died.

Second, the old adage, "Keep your friends close and your enemies closer," was made for Alan, as those who fell on his bad side usually paid a horrible price. It was a matter of self-preservation that dictated that it was best to keep him on your good side. Now that he had become involved with The Cult of the Disillusioned, I really had no choice but to interact with him, considering that he had become one of our biggest and most steady financial contributors.

One of the most self-satisfied, egocentric game players I have ever known, Alan had a way of subtly reminding a person that he was the one in control. One example among many, Alan once owned a theater I performed in, and as a birthday gift, he presented the director with a marionette puppet that had $100 bills taped to its hands and feet, as well as one taped to the crotch. Reminding the director that he basically owned him, this was what one could expect from Alan, who was always the snake in the grass ready to strike at any moment. His money and criminal position made him a formidable force to be reckoned with, and many in town rightly feared him.

Susan, having her own history with Alan, had become concerned about Sky and Alan bedding down together as well, and the fact that we lacked a proper tracking system of the money that was pouring in from everywhere worried her, especially when the church decided to go for a loan. When stressed, Susan became distant and quiet, and due to her high position in the church, she didn't feel it was her place to gossip. We just found it easier to just look away.

The meeting with Alan was not easy, and I had taken Tristan to the restaurant with me for moral support. Not able to fully grasp the history between us—or that with Alan what you saw was never even close to what you received—Tristan found Alan's reputation fascinating and was eager to meet the man behind the legend. Unable to get the image out of my head of the last gift I received from Alan, which was the towel filled with David's brain and skull fragments, I vowed that this time I would keep Alan as far away from me as I could.

The meeting with Alan was strange as always. He spent a great deal of time staring at me while asking Tristan questions regarding me as if I wasn't there. Asking how we met, probing to see how much Tristan knew of my past, it was almost as if Alan was trying to ascertain whether or not I was talking about things I had previously been warned to keep silent about. The only questions posed to me concerned my relationship with Sky and the problems I had with him, unnerving me that he knew so much about our conflict. (Of course, now I know that Fred was talking to Alan about me, but I didn't realize that then.)

I felt as if I was being set up, so I did my best to respond vaguely, assuring him that the church was solid as was my commitment to it, despite any misgivings I might have about

Sky. Finally, Alan handed me a check for $500, already made out to Sky. Smiling, he wished me luck, then got up and walked out.

This was the first of many experiences with Alan during our stay at The Cult of the Disillusioned. Each time would be equally strange, building up to a breaking point that would eventually cause Tristan and me to break from the church. Fixated on Tristan, Alan would follow us, but that was later.

A dry drunk, Sky couldn't escape his past profession, and the bigger the church got, the more Sky turned Sunday's services into a lounge act. All that was missing was an open bar. In hopes of getting on television, Sky's sermons became more and more obscure, finally ending up as a "let's all feel good" philosophy. Sky and his posse dominated the church, and those voicing any dissent were quickly silenced and run out.

Dr. Smith often listened in disbelief to the things I told her were happening in the church, concerned that I was once again placing myself in chaotic situations in order to repeat behaviors I was in therapy trying to correct. But I was not yet willing to walk away. I felt a sense of community within the church, and I tried to reassure myself it wasn't all bad.

As Sky's right-hand person with regard to the land campaign, Susan had to work with Alan Baer as well, finding the experience as intolerable as I. Sharing our stories about Alan, we discovered that the two of us had more in common than we thought, as she had run with a group of Baer Boys when she was a teenager and knew more about the early gay bar scene than I did.

I don't think anyone foresaw what was coming next for The Cult of the Disillusioned, but I think it is safe to say that it caught everyone off guard. This was the first time I'd ever seen Alan take it up the butt himself, as Sky was about to show just how strong his propensity to create chaos was, and, in the end, we would all find ourselves spinning in the winds he unleashed.

FURTHER JOURNEYS

I was furthering my studies in Shamanism while being healed in the process. Working with my inner consciousness, I was beginning to expand my worldview and how I looked at life, and it was having a calming effect on me. Always working within the context of what I understood, my journeys, in the beginning, were very frightening. My first attempt with practicing Shamanism was the worst, although the journeys I would experience after my father's death would be even more frightening.

Immediately after my soul retrieval with Cathy, I decided not to wait for the upcoming introductory class to see if I could actually journey myself. Alone in my apartment, I lit some incense, said some prayers for protection and guidance, and as my stereo drummed I laid down, closed my eyes, and waited to see what would happen.

The drumming had a calming effect, and, drifting away on the incense, I let my mind go, allowing myself to daydream. As my imagination swept me away, I became a bystander much like I would have if I were actually dreaming. Practicing shamanism is like a form of self-hypnosis, with a strong emphasis on self-help and strengthening the psyche.

I began by visualizing a safe place in my mind to begin my journey. Michael Harner in *The Way of the Shaman* explained that to get to the upper world, you simply had to picture yourself going through a hole in the sky. It is in this realm that you are able to meet ancestors, guides, and angels, all of whom offer guidance and support.

To access the lower world, which primarily deals with healing, you would do the opposite, finding a hole you could go *down* into, like the rabbit hole described in *Alice in Wonderland*. Using the imagery of following down the roots of a tree, or swimming to the bottom of the ocean or a lake, it was explained that you should imagine going down and coming out into the lower world on the other side.

For me, the lower world is always forested and shadowy, not in a bad way but rather like when the vegetation blocks out the sun. Full of lakes and forests, the lower world I found was peaceful and serene. It is in the lower world that shamans believe you can connect with spirit guides who are represented as animals. Shamans focusing on the spirits don't *become* the animal they imagine so much as they try to take on the animal's attributes, trying to derive a personal sense of awareness in the process. For example, Bear energy heals me, Wolf energy commands, Spider energy captivates, and so on. As a result, shamans believe that the lessons of the universe can always be found in nature.

The middle world is the most dangerous and the hardest to navigate because it is connected to the material plane in a way the other two aren't. It is the realm within which we all live, connected to the power of both heaven and hell. The middle world contains pockets of concentrated negative energy, and it is where some of the dead are trapped, particularly those who, while alive, lacked clear concepts of right and wrong, thus getting caught up in experiences they were unable to release at death.

One of the most important tools of the shamanic trade is the ability to help such spirits cross over into the light. Only an adept shaman is able to safely navigate these invisible perils of the middle world.

Perhaps because of my past, I ended up in the middle world during my first journey, (coincidentally happening, unbeknownst to me at the time, on a night we also had a record meteor shower). Standing beside an angel, I found myself in the midst of the Big Bang. Entire planets flew past us out into the universe as if they were nothing, and, as it is in dreams, the angel informed me that I was part of the stardust making up all the life in the universe.

Terrified, I ended the journey as soon as I started it by ripping off the blindfold that was over my eyes. And there I was, confronted by a sight I will never forget.

I found myself surrounded by a crowd of beings that I could only surmise were ghosts. Never having seen a ghost before, I saw their iridescent outlines in the darkened room, crowding around me, and although I vaguely believed in ghosts, I had never seen one, let alone a group of them. I screamed and dodged for the lights, freaked out in a way hard to explain.

Once again, I was alone in the room, frightened. What exactly had I experienced?

I immediately called Cathy. Believing every word, amazed at the intensity of my first journey given that many people are generally unsuccessful with the first few tries, she believed I had seen the universe reaching a point of rebirth. Having been a shaman for years, she found my experience of being surrounded by spirits significant and asked me if I knew why they were there. Intuiting it was because they were proud of what I was doing, or at least that's how it felt, Cathy encouraged me to further myself in the practice.

Journeying for me was a natural transition away from Satanism, although vastly different in practice. An interesting contrast between Shamanism and Satanism concerns a practice shamans call the *dismemberment journey*. My family's satanic friends took the ritual of dismemberment of others very seriously, but shamans derive a much different sense of power in their own dismemberment.

In a visionary state, I was once eaten by a swarm of piranhas in a journey; another time I was ripped apart by crows. Ancient myths are filled with the theme of hero dismemberment, stories in which the soul is "ripped apart" so it can be rebuilt and transformed. For centuries, satanists have distorted this psychic transformation into something literal and pernicious. However, each time I underwent a shamanic dismemberment journey, something from my past would fall away and transform into something better than before, strengthening me in the process.

In many respects, I was just applying what Aquino's mind-control practices taught me as a child, but I learned to take it much further than the communing with demons he had interest in, although I wouldn't realize it at the time.

Dr. Smith was interested in knowing whether a shamanic respect for the dream could help me with my chronic nightmares that often robbed me of restful sleep.

A GREAT UNVEILING

When someone asks me if I truly believe shamanism works, I like to relate the story of when Susan and I attended a weekend seminar on death and dying. Being a marvelous visionary in her own right, she was rapidly finding strength in her spirituality and had begun to blossom in the church, graduating from the friendly but shy fly on the wall to the confident, intelligent, involved woman I always knew she was.

The land campaign had been going splendidly and she was proud of the fact that she alone had brought in hundreds of thousands of dollars to help purchase the new land for the new church, off Seventy-Second Street, north of Immanuel Hospital.

She arrived at the seminar distraught. She had spent weeks preparing the paperwork for the bank loan to finance the land, and she had gone to the church at six the previous morning, feeling quite nervous about the meeting with the bank later that day. To her surprise, she found Sky in her office changing numbers on the loan request by hundreds of thousands of dollars. The piece of land we were looking at was prime real estate, and the million and a half we were buying it for was a steal.

Caught off guard, Susan explained that Sky told her that he was making some last-minute changes that they needed to keep to themselves. During the meeting with the bank, Sky dominated the proceedings, not allowing Susan to say a word. The numbers failed to meet the bank's expectations and the loan was denied. Susan had finally experienced Sky's corruption firsthand and was beside herself.

The universe drew us together as we both were taking the same weekend class on the shamanic practice of "psycho-pumping." We were learning the practice of communing with the dead in the middle world—the one in which we all live and call reality—and helping them to the other side. By this time, I'd taken basic and advanced classes in shamanism and was fairly knowledgeable as to how it worked.

That first day, we were asked to go to a place in our minds where someone had died and see what would happen. Thinking of my friend David, I went (mentally) to the apartment where he was murdered and found him standing in the kitchen. Sensing my presence, he turned and demanded to know what I was doing there. Then a light appeared and standing within it was David's old lover who had died of AIDS a few years before. Recognizing his partner, David walked into the light, leaving me standing alone in the apartment.

I ended the journey feeling rejected and disheartened, wishing that David had been happier to see me and given that I was still struggling with having never gotten the chance to apologize to him, I figured my mind was playing out a scenario that I believed *would* have happened, had it happened for "real."

The next morning, as I was preparing to return to the next seminar, I walked into my sewing room and saw the nametag from David's military jacket sitting in my trash basket. BJ had given me the jacket after David's death, and I'd removed the nametag when the jacket didn't fit me anymore, storing it in a box in my upstairs closet, yet, somehow, there was the nametag, and I had absolutely no idea of how it got in the trash.

I reached down to retrieve it and was suddenly struck by an image in my mind that I had pulled our friendship out of the trash. Tears sprang to my eyes as I realized that it was a message from David, telling me in a way that my apology had been accepted.

Events, however, didn't end there.

The day before we had divided the seminar room in half, planning to try to psycho-pump the next day as a group. Susan chose the group who decided to focus mentally on an airplane crash that had personally affected a woman in the class to see if they could find any spirits needing help in crossing over. Looking back, in a way, the airplane crash would become symbolic of The Cult of the Disillusioned and a sign of things to come for Susan.

My group chose to mentally go to the apartment I had rented after my mother's death, which was near the Gerald Ford Memorial. We'd been having a lot of paranormal activity in our apartment—lights going on and off, hearing people walk around at night, watching our dogs become agitated and bark at empty rooms. Even Tristan, a nonbeliever, was having a hard time explaining what was happening. So our two groups planned our journeys for the next day.

The next afternoon, after my group journeyed to our apartment, I decided to just sit and listen to what everyone had to say, figuring since it was my apartment that it would be best for me to listen rather than share what I'd experienced. I wanted to hear others' experiences without influencing them in any way.

Remarkably, each contributor described correctly the layout of the apartment, as well as discerned a problem with spirits. They viewed our apartment as a sort of Grand Central Station of spirits. More interesting, each who spoke also saw Tristan lying on the couch watching television.

Immediately during the next break, I called Tristan and asked what he was doing at that very moment. He admitted he was lying in his underwear on the couch in the living room, watching television and talking on the phone, activities he normally did not do.

When I told him that the entire group had seen him in the apartment, we were *both* taken aback, but when he came to pick me up, he was further shocked when people in my group recognized him and complimented him on his cute, hairy legs. Having no idea how it was possible they could have seen him, he couldn't deny the fact that it happened, and the experience gave both of us a better appreciation of shamanism.

Travel in the middle world or to any of the three realms of the spiritual world is also known as astral projection or directing the spirit out of the body in order to explore what the spiritual world has to offer. Through the mind, journeys require faith in yourself and in God. As the death and dying seminar proved, God has a way of offering the universe's own sense of "proof" that some prefer to call coincidence. In my experience, coincidence after coincidence is called a pattern, and throughout my practice I've begun to see definite patterns.

There is no doubt that shamanism works within the mental framework of the practitioner, as visions within dream states are the primary focus of our practice. Eventually, I learned how to travel back into my dreams once awake in order to psychically change them, which helped to take the fear out of my nightmares.

Mentally changing the outcome of the dreams meant emotionally and mentally changing the energy associated with them, which helped me to garner more stability, and I worked at freeing myself from the psychological shackles I found so disturbing when I was awake.

A week after the seminar, Sky ran Susan out of the church. He referred to her as "evil" and blamed his actions with the loan papers on her "ineffectiveness," despite the fact that the money we had was largely a result of her diligence. His right-hand person one day and his public enemy the next, Susan gave up and left the church.

Sky's ex, a demanding perfectionist who fashioned himself sort of an Anne Rice character Vampire Lestat in overly laced blouses, had already taken over the music and the band. With Alan's help, Sky and Sunday services hit cable access. Rumors were circulating about Fred having inappropriate contact with minors in the church, and though I did not want to believe them, Fred's jokes about fifteen-year-old boys made them sound sadly plausible.

A special town hall meeting was called to discuss how to deal with the allegations, at which Fred was glaringly absent. Many felt it was inappropriate for the church to be discussing such things in public, but it was a sign of things to come.

Alan invited me to dine with him and his wife at their home in Fairacres. The home was lavishly and impeccably decorated with rooms of Asian art. Both his wife and their house were beautiful and Marsha, his wife, was incredibly charming. A powerhouse in her own right, she was a Brandeis, from a very old-moneyed family.

Devoutly Jewish, she was definitely not ignorant of Alan's true nature, but according to Fred, their marriage was very convenient. She didn't care for Sky and considered him a snake oil salesman. Marsha Baer was brutally honest, like my mother, and I found her refreshing and wondered what the hell she saw in Alan.

At a Christmas party one year, Sky stood up and exclaimed that our church was the loosest church in town and since everyone had been drinking, we'd all better stay, never knowing what could happen. I stared at my plate while Alan sat at our table, bragging about how he'd gotten out of the Franklin thing years before by manipulating the money from his foundation in Omaha.

Laughing about his invincibility, he alluded to killing people by bragging how easy it was to dispose of problems if you had the knowhow. Tristan and I left immediately after dinner, and I ended up vomiting the rest of the night, unable to get Alan's smirk out of my mind.

After Susan left the church, it was my turn, given that I knew the real story as to why the loan had failed. First, Sky made an executive decision to replace me as head of Gifts from the Heart, effectively removing me from the cookbook sales. Tristan, by this time, had had enough and started talking about how it was time to let The Cult of the Disillusioned go, along with the cookbook I'd spent so much time producing. Then Sky disbanded Gifts from the Heart all together, and I walked away from the community I'd once felt so passionate about, feeling beaten once again.

Six months later, Sky left the church to return to Hawaii to begin another divide-and-conquer ministry in another cheated church, leaving Alan high and dry. Never knowing the whole story between the two, but judging from what he said around town, it was obvious that Alan felt slighted. I vowed never to return to the church, even with Sky gone.

Alan was, at this time, dying of prostate cancer, but even though he was distracted by his roller coaster ride of doctors and recommendations as he fought for more life, and though he was starting to look frail, I knew he was as evil as ever.

I had one last opportunity to tell Alan what I thought of him at dinner one night, after he tried to separate Tristan and me by offering Tristan a job.

"I feel sorry for you," I started out.

He looked at me, "Why?"

"If you were a grocery store clerk, nobody would look twice at you. So you don't know if people actually love you or if they love what you can do for them," I said. "And that must be very lonely."

As he looked at me to respond, he hesitated, stood up, grabbed his coat from the back of the chair, and stormed out.

Alan Baer died in November 2002, eaten alive by his own anus—a fitting death for a man who had screwed so many.

> Philanthropist Alan Baer Dies, November 6, 2002, *Omaha World-Herald* (p. 1b): Baer, 79, died of cancer Tuesday afternoon. ... "He was one of the warmest, and generous human beings I've ever met," [Jeffrey] Silver said. [Silver was identified in the story as a friend and family lawyer.] "He had a great sense of humor and treated everyone with respect."

12

SKELETONS IN THE CLOSET

lthough laborious and painful, therapy was going well. I could now identify and change the behaviors I was unhappy with, but it took an inordinate amount of work and time. Still, I kept at it, figuring that the only way to curb my acting out unconsciously was to plod onward, exploring my thoughts and feelings as to why I saw life the way I did, thus strengthening my sense of consciousness and self-awareness.

Tristan was growing sick of hearing about my infidelities with strangers and had at last begun holding me accountable, confronting me when he was angry or unhappy. I realized that anyone else would have left me long ago. I knew Tristan loved me in a way I wasn't used to.

As for the Antichrist obsession, a friend of mine cut me down to size when she remarked: "You're the Antichrist? You? What are you going to do, insult people on their clothing choices? The minute they cry, you will too, so you won't make much of an Antichrist."

Still worried that I would become like my father, her comment helped to ease my fears, and now whenever I think back on her comment, I laugh. Dr. Smith was convinced that the Antichrist conviction came from my family doing their best to pigeonhole me into playing the bad guy. Often reminding me that I wasn't as crazy as I thought, she hoped I could overcome the effects of the trauma through mental exploration of memories and reliving the feelings associated with those memories.

She would do this in a safe place where she could guide me in letting the past go. I always wondered if she believed me or not, but she once told me that she found me to be neither crazy nor a liar and suggested that I take that for what it was worth.

Shamanic seminars were few and far between, and The Cult of the Disillusioned was history, so I once again found myself alone. My faith wasn't any less, but I was putting it on the back burner, as faith takes work, and I was tired of worrying about God. I was disabled and out of work, with an abundance of time on my hands, which resulted in the perfect conditions for the idle mind to become the Devil's playground.

It was a late winter's night when I finally got busted in the park, which turned out to be a blessing in disguise.

It was a frigid January night after the Christmas I wrote the letter to my father. I had driven to Elmwood Park after midnight so that I could smoke my last joint. I had begun trying to convince myself that the sexual abuse I remembered as a child had either not been so bad, or never happened. Unable to face the emotional consequences of my de-masculinization, I found myself in constant limbo, and often thinking about my father and our past, all I wanted to do was get high and escape.

Denial is strong in those who've experienced great trauma, and it was especially true for me. I found it more comfortable to tell myself that I was crazy rather than to consider the implications of what had happened to me, so I spent inordinate amounts of time trying to escape the memories that constantly intruded on me. Desperately lonely, my mother and the church gone, I spiraled down into the hands of the law.

A man pulled up in a big blue pickup exactly like the one my father drove when he worked for a propane company. In a ball cap, clean-shaven with a mustache, he was the spitting image of my father when he was younger. He lowered his window and asked what I was up to and if I wanted to go for a ride.

Uncomfortable, I agreed to meet him on the darker side of the park closer to the road. Long story short, I got in and out of his truck twice, unable to escape him for reasons I couldn't understand. Adamant about sex, he kept asking me if I wanted to blow him or if I wanted him to blow me. Wanting neither, but not wanting to hurt his feelings, I ended up suggesting to him we meet later in the parking lot of a nearby grocery store, which is what got me busted.

I had had more sex than I could remember in the parks, but on this particular night I was neither looking for nor wanting sex, but I felt captivated by the man who reminded me of my father, and feeling like a child, I was unable to remove myself from a situation I knew was wrong. Like a deer caught in the headlights, although free to leave at any time, I was nonetheless unable to extricate myself from the situation.

Feeling, in the end, like I'd been set up, I became angry and argued with the undercover cop while he wrote me a ticket for soliciting sex. He responded by telling me that men only came to the parks for one reason, and though I knew that wasn't always true, I couldn't escape the feeling that karma had come to bite me in the ass. I accepted the ticket, left the park, lit my joint, and drove home.

The next day while talking with Dr. Smith, I had an especially hard time dealing with the fact that even though I had wanted to escape the situation several times, I had felt frozen, unable to do anything other than what I was told.

She explained that it was common for victims of abuse to find themselves creating situations loosely based on their original trauma, which caused them to feel as immobilized as they did as children. Although inappropriate, my behavior was understandable considering what I had experienced as a child, and she felt that much could be derived from the experience if I was willing to honestly explore it.

I tried, in court, to challenge what I considered to be entrapment. I speculated that what had happened to me was happening to men all over town, perhaps as a backlash against the gay-dominated days of the 1980s. Omaha had begun a no-tolerance-for-homosexuality campaign, and the police were busting up to four hundred men a summer in parks such as Elmwood, Mandan, and Cunningham around town. Names were published in the paper, and police proposed to put the names up on a billboard. Several men committed suicide as a result, after their lives were publically destroyed.

Everyone in my life knew about the charges I was facing as I was living a policy of forthrightness and told everyone, and although I was guilty of having sex in the parks in the past, knowing on that night I had no such intention, I started out fighting the charges. My public defender discovered the cop had been caught lying in court before, trying to set people up, but that was never introduced in court.

I ended up pleading no contest after being told there was no way out of the charges. Avoiding court costs, I was told to pay a $98 fine, which at least kept my name out of the news. It is one of the most humiliating experiences of my life, although I have to say that I am glad for two reasons that it happened.

First, the bust forced a desperately needed clarification for me. Projecting my dad onto the policeman, thus putting me back into the mindset of a child, reminded me of how *powerless* I had felt at the time. The shame of my vulnerability became viable, and the experience helped remind me that the fear I felt for my father had been real and not something I had made up in my child mind. As a result, I was able to explore buried feelings associated with my father and the trauma associated with our relationship.

The second reason, although it wouldn't be until years later, is that the experience gave me the chance to reach out and get closer to Art—the victim of a crime himself. Art had been abducted and held hostage for three days by an escaped rapist (who had tricked his guards with a papier-mâché gun made from the cardboard middle of a toilet paper roll).

Having stolen a realistic toy gun by this point, the escapee from the Nebraska Correctional Center tricked Art into his own apartment and tied him up to his bed. Three days later, while the guy was out of the house, Art was able to phone the police by dialing with a pencil held in his teeth. The police apprehended the escaped convict after a shootout a few blocks from Art's apartment, then later broke into the apartment and untied Art.

Never having really understood my trouble with PTSD, Art gained a whole new appreciation for my plight in life, and we often spoke of his traumatizing experience and how it had emotionally affected him.

Had I not experienced such entrapment with the undercover cop in the park, I might never have known such an important aspect about myself, and I certainly wouldn't have been able to share Art's suffering regarding his own vulnerability. I regret having wasted so much of my life in the parks, but I do not regret being busted. It was the wake-up call I had needed—an undeniable demonstration of the fact that I was losing control and seeking refuge in denial.

Within the context of therapy, Dr. Smith and I examined each nuance that caused me to fill the void inside with strangers. Reminding me that the only thing we are able to truly control is ourselves, and that the only constant in life is change, by delving deep into my psyche, I came to see that my life needed serious change that could only be achieved by intensely focusing on my behavior and the reasons behind it.

FACING MY PAST

Looking back, I see now that people like my father and oldest sister didn't want me exploring my past or giving it a great deal of thought because they didn't want me digging around in my own head.

My quest for discovery made them uncomfortable, and although they watched over me and constantly encouraged me to forget my past and walk away, they couldn't explain to me why. Having grown used to keeping silent, not wanting to weird anyone out with the horror stories of my past, I never assumed an ulterior motive behind anyone's actions other than my story made them uncomfortable. Sooner than expected, my luxury of denial would end; I would discover that they all had their reasons.

I began to explore my artistic side, after discovering I had proficiency with a sewing machine. I set up a studio in our home, and having nothing better to do, I started making wall hangings. I had grown tired of my endless summer vacation lifestyle and felt that I needed something to occupy my time or I would end up going back to my pursuit of sexual encounters. I channeled my energy into my art rather than dwelling on the skeletons in my family closet, in order to avoid getting caught up in their constant chaos.

Dr. Smith helped me to understand the confusion I felt at being pulled in so many directions with regard to my family. Our sessions exposed the raw anger I felt toward my mother, as well as the anger I felt with myself. Patiently, Dr. Smith explained again and again that my parents' choices were not my fault while suggesting the idea that I had choices as an adult that I didn't have as a child.

I was scared that I'd end up like them, figuring the nut doesn't fall far from the tree. But Dr. Smith assured me that I was nothing like my parents. Often massaging this recurrent fear, she explained that although the nut may not fall far from the tree, it is often picked up by birds, squirrels, and the wind and carried farther than the little nut could ever imagine. This simple analogy made sense and helped me to accept that it was not my fate to become like my father.

I would further realize the truth of this when my father paid for Cindy and Stephen to come to Omaha to see him before he died. At the time, no one was really speaking to Sarah, and I wasn't speaking to Stephen. We spent most of our lives estranged from each other, and this time was no different.

My brother and stepmother were concerned with what my father was saying on his deathbed, which explained their incessant need to discredit him, as they tried to prevent anyone from listening to him expound on revealing family secrets.

The night my stepmother took my brother to the airport, I coincidentally called my father's house at the same time to talk to Cindy in order to make plans to see her before she left. Suddenly, our father grabbed the phone from her and tearfully begged me to come and see him, declaring that he had something to tell me. He refused to give my sister back the phone until I swore that I would come immediately. My sister was as surprised as I.

The sight of him sitting on the couch in the living room took me aback. No longer the oppressive, domineering man I remembered as a child, he had now become a frail, sad individual who looked deeply troubled.

The second I walked into his living room, my dad said, "I've read your letter more times than I can count and it's made me do a lot of thinking," at which point he looked me straight in the eye and made the declaration, "I have skeletons in my closet."

Cindy instantly went pale, but remained sitting beside him silently. I would later discover that she had turned white due to the fact that she knew what he was trying to tell me, but all I could do was stare at him. Concerned with the direction that the conversation was headed, and seeing the effect it was having on Cindy, I tried to placate him by responding, "I know, Dad."

He grew visibly agitated and tried unsuccessfully to rise from his chair. He leaned forward and loudly proclaimed: "You don't understand. I have *skeletons* in my closet."

"Can we talk about this later?" I asked. I was concerned for Cindy's sake. She was visibly becoming upset and had just been released from the hospital.

Later, broaching the subject with Sarah, she commented how he'd said the same thing to her when she'd dropped by with a friend a week before, using the exact same words. Figuring that he was talking about all the stuff from our childhood, she'd shut him down the same way I did, declaring that she didn't want to discuss the past and that, as far as she was concerned, all was forgiven.

I have often regretted not letting him explain exactly what he was talking about. If I had one moment of my life to live over again, changing the outcome, it would be that one. His words would plague me after he died. In fact, they still do, especially considering he had completely rebuilt their bedroom closet (presumably and literally to conceal dead kids) along with a platform bed and strangely enough had had a sound-proof room installed in their house in the laundry room years before.

THE ARCHANGEL URIEL

I saw my father one last time, a couple weeks before he died. Wanting to assure him that when he died I would come find him and help him cross over, I hoped to comfort him so that he wouldn't be so scared to face his mortality. Despite everything, I loved my father and had grown to feel sorry for his life much like I had with my mom. It was the last time I would see him on this side.

Three days before he died, I began having nightmares about a demon. I found myself standing in the kitchen of our old apartment, all the doors leading to the living room and dining room were shut tight, and I could hear something slithering around on the other side of the door, making a sound like nails scratching on glass.

Suddenly, there was a knock at the front door, and I could hear a woman entering the apartment. She was attacked by the demon, and her screams and those of the demon awakened me in a panic. The next several nights, the nightmare repeated itself over and over, always the same except that it was always a different woman at the door.

Of course, I had plenty of nightmares, but this one was different in that it felt so *real*, and its constant repetition felt as if the universe was trying to tell me something. Dr. Smith suggested that I use my shamanic practice to go into the dream while awake to see if there was anything I could do, as I was becoming afraid to close my eyes and was losing sleep.

Unaware that my father was dying, I didn't equate the dream with my past, nor could I ever have imagined what was about to happen.

On the third morning, after two nights of nightmares, Cindy phoned and told me that our father had died. I spent the rest of the day trying to make sense of my feelings, because I seemed to feel nothing. He was an enigma. I loved my father as much as I despised everything he stood for. His satanic past aside, he'd grown to be a narcissistic, selfish, deceitful person who had done immense harm in his life, and it was difficult to dismiss the pain he'd caused just because he had passed. True to my word, I still had every intention of finding him on the other side and helping him cross over.

Shamans believe that after physical death the soul goes through a process of letting go of the ties that bound it to its previous life. Although space and time are irrelevant on the other side, the soul is believed to still be bound within the confines of common reality during this transition, thus the process requires at least three days to complete. Considering that Jesus Christ himself took three days to ascend, shamans give the soul that time to deal with its loss while reacquainting itself with the other side.

I decided to give my father ten days, considering how my father was the angry, spiteful, and bitter man he was, hiding "skeletons in his closet." Figuring it would be best to give him some extra time to try and make amends on the other side, I had no idea that my own soul would be on the line before I would ever get a chance to help him.

The morning after he died, I found myself possessed by the very demon we had believed resided in my father. Unlike anything I had ever experienced, I heard a terrible voice in my head say, *You're not like the others.* Shamans, like satanists, believe in possession, which is the whole reason behind praying for protection before journeying. Leaving the body unprotected can open it to possession by spirits, but I had never experienced it, and even with my background as it was, I didn't really understand how it was possible.

Just the week before, I had laughed at a friend of ours, a staunch Catholic, after he commented on how scary he found the film *The Exorcism of Emily Rose* to be. Although he was terrified by the concept of how the Devil can possess the bodies of mere mortals, I scoffed at him, explaining that the true story ended with the girl's parents and priest going to jail for starving the girl to death. Going further, I assured him that possession was silly, surmising that demons had better things to do than possess humans, yet now, here I was, facing the very thing I had mocked.

Even though I was assured that this would happen as a child, nothing could have prepared me for the actual experience, and I spent my time trying to deny the experience even while it was happening.

In my mind all I could sense was a being that seemed all eyes and tongues. Desperate, angry, and extremely powerful, I began having flashes of life memories as the thing searched my mind, looking for something to entice me with. As it looked into me, I could see into him, and I sensed that he was both incredibly old and incredibly sad.

I had never encountered such a hopeless being in all my journeys, but I wasn't so much scared as intrigued, because this seemed to be the moment I'd been prepared for as a child. The being told me that I could do anything in this life now and never face a day's consequence for what I did. I felt an incredible surge of power from him, though with it also came an overwhelming sense of corruption.

Instinctively, I knew that the thing inside of me was offering more of the same darkness I had been trying to escape for decades. Afterward, perhaps exhausted by the transition from my father to me, I felt it curl up like a snake, much like it was asleep, still inside me but silent.

I called my shaman friend Susan immediately and detailed for her what I had just experienced. She explained a shamanic process called extractment, which, in many ways, sounded a lot like exorcism. Though not common, it was also not impossible, and Susan told me of a practicing shaman in town who specialized in extractment. She suggested I call him and ask for his help.

At first, Dr. Smith was unsure as to what to suggest, but she did her best to help me explore the demonic experience in our next session. It could just be some sort of programming playing out, she suggested, or may be due to the fact I had always been told it would happen when my father died. Nevertheless, she assured me that she didn't believe I was crazy. Schizophrenics hear voices *outside* their heads, not inside, so she did her best to convince me that I wasn't having a psychotic break, which was what I was convinced was happening.

Believing there would be no harm in letting it play out, she suggested that I take Susan's advice and undergo the extractment to see what would happen.

That afternoon, I called my sister Cindy and told her what was happening and what I intended to do. Remember: we were all raised to believe that something dwelled in my father, and although I was the only one who had any form of spiritual training by way of shamanism, each of us possessed our own abilities. Cindy was convinced that if I released the demon inside of me, we would lose our "powers."

Both of my sisters were adept with the occult; at times they saw visions of the future along with their own versions of psychic powers. Cindy could look into people's lives and see what troubled them, as could Sarah, who was also a fantastic tarot card reader, and although we had all denied our abilities at certain points in our lives, all of us had been shaped by our experiences as children and, as such, believed in the powers of magic and the spiritual world, as well as in the demon that had gone out of my father and into me.

That night before bed, I prayed for an answer to my dilemma, awaking the next morning knowing what I had to do. Back in my studio, I began talking out loud, feeling stupid but not caring. Having no dreams or nightmares that I remembered, I nonetheless woke with the knowledge of whom I was dealing with, where he had come from, and why he was here.

"Your name is Uriel, is it not? The one we worshiped when I was a child?" I asked.

Answering, *That I am,* I went further and asked:

"And you have to do anything I ask of you, no matter what it is?"

You need only to command me. I could taste his anticipation, sensing that his humility was a trick.

"Since you have to do anything I want you to do, no matter what it is, then what I want is for you to go to God and ask what it is God wants you to do, and then I want you to do that instead."

Caught off guard, he was bound nonetheless by my request, and having no other option than to honor it, he became silent and we didn't speak further.

Not quite understanding exactly what was happening, I realized that, real or not, I had no interest in using this being. Having awakened that morning aware of his overwhelming sense of hopelessness based on his belief that he would never be able to return to the light, I knew that the being within me was willing to burn the world down in order to force the hand of God in hopes of ending his suffering.

Think about it. Jesus preached that God is love, commanding us to forgive and love our enemies, all the while God plans to throw his enemies into an eternal fire pit. Does that make sense? Knowing that no one can thwart the will of God, and believing that God will wait until the end of time for all of the flock to return, I felt it was time for this being to see the truth.

Not comprehending at the time how this experience was connected to my past, I did what I could to get through it while trying to keep both my sanity and soul intact.

I called the local shaman and set up an extractment. The sense that Uriel was inside me was undeniable. Crazy or not, I felt I had to play it out, no matter how weird it was.

In the book *Cult and Ritual Abuse: Its History, Anthropology, and Recent Discovery in Contemporary America,* James Randall Noblitt and Pamela Sue Perskin talk about the connection between possession, ritual abuse, and dissociation on page 44. Quoting Father Jeffery Steffon from his 1992 book *Satanism: Is It Real,* they give the Catholic Church's official position regarding the reality of Satan, evil spirits, and demonic possession. Citing Father Richard McAlear and Betty Brennan, experts on demonic possession, Father Steffon explains that the church believes possession occurs

... through a person's generational heritage. People inherit their make-up from their parents—their physical attributes, mental abilities, psychological makeup, and spiritual characteristics. If parents have been involved in the occult, generational openness for the oppression will be passed along to their children. Exodus 20:5-6 states that a father's wickedness is passed on to his children for four generations, but blessings for a thousand generations upon the faithful. Finally, a demonic spirit can attach itself to a person through involvement in the occult.

No wonder I found myself in the position I was in. Still avoiding delving too far into my past, I figured that I would do the extractment and that would be the end of it, and I was looking forward to reclaiming my life, especially considering the fact that my parents were dead. Unconcerned as to whether this was a true spiritual experience or one that my fractured mind was using to repair itself, I was willing to do what I had to do to get over what I felt was a precipice.

A SHAMANIC EXTRACTMENT

The local shaman was nicknamed Bear, and for good reason. His size, dark hair, and beard made him look like a big grizzly. He ushered me into their living room where prayer blankets had been draped over everything. He explained they were hung to keep spirits from attaching themselves to objects during the extractment.

He took a moment to get a feel for me and to ask how much I knew about the extractment process. Admitting I knew virtually nothing about it and that it all seemed strange to me, he took my ignorance in stride, pointing out that whether I believed in what was happening or not, the fact remained I was still sitting in his house. Laughing, he told me that people who experienced what I was often had a hard time believing what was happening, but assured me that it was very real.

The ceremony itself was simple. Bear lit a candle, burned some incense, and prayed over me and the area of the extractment, not much different than what Cathy had done during my soul extractment. Asking for help from the other side, he prayed and sang as he beat a drum, walking around me in a circle as I sat on the floor. Finally, he sat down in front of me and told me to stare into his eyes. I had felt myself already beginning to drift when Bear asked me to mentally move to the side and allow Uriel to take over my body. His wife, sitting beside him, quietly said prayers as Bear provoked the demon into talking.

The experience of listening to myself talk was strange in that the words weren't coming from me. There was no speaking in tongues, projectile green vomit, nor any other theatric generally associated with exorcism, but instead a kind of grace fell upon the room that made the air almost glow around us. I could feel

Uriel's hesitation and fear, but because he was bound to my request, he had no choice but to cross over. Anxious to be rid of him, I still found myself tearing up, and I felt a sense of loss but not a clue as to why, although I was soon to learn the answer.

Bear helped Uriel to the other side but how he did it I still don't understand. Physically feeling Uriel leave me, I breathed a sigh of relief as Bear looked at his wife, asking her if we were done. Somehow working in conjunction with her husband, she was visibly surprised when she answered "no." It was at this point that I felt the presence of someone I realized had been with me since childhood. Telling Bear that there was a woman inside of me, Bear's wife then looked at me and told me I had to let her go.

Suddenly I felt overwhelmed with love from the female presence inside me. I realized that my tears had been for her. Dr. Smith had often asked me how I had overcome my childhood, and I told her about the voice I heard as a child, constantly assuring me that everything was okay and it was the people around me who were crazy, not me. I believed all those years that the voice was a part of me, but I now realize that I had help in getting through the hell of my childhood.

This spirit dwelled within me, and it had been her voice that I had heard in my head all those years. Knowing it was time for her to leave and cross over, I felt an overwhelming gratitude toward her for the love she had shared with me through my loveless childhood. I envisioned her gently brushing her hand against my cheek as I felt her leave me and cross over. Then it was over.

Bear finished with another prayer ceremony, and while beating his drum and thanking God and the universe for its help, he sang praise and thanks as his wife continued to quietly pray.

He explained that it was customary for the shaman to send the "patient" home with gifts, so he sent me home with some wood from a Joshua tree he'd come across in his travels, a packet with corn and tree shavings in it, and a crystal that, in a way, looked like a village.

Native Americans, he said, believe you are never poor as long as you have a couple of grains of corn in the cupboard. He told me that the packet was for my sister Cindy, who he sensed was having the hardest time with our father's death.

He too was amazed by how easy Uriel's transition had gone and confirmed that Uriel was not only ancient and probably on the Earth since before the days of Mesopotamia, he was also the most powerful being Bear had ever encountered. He was amazed that the whole process had gone as easy as it did and that the demon didn't fight (which was generally the case), but knowing that Uriel was bound by my request, I understood. Exhausted and sad, feeling as if I'd lost a piece of me and emotionally confused by the whole experience, I thanked Bear and his wife and bid farewell.

Later that night, lying in bed, I felt as if I had just passed a crucial test. The evil no longer inside of me, I wondered what might have happened had I ignored his presence and gone about my daily affairs. I let the scenario play out in my mind until I thought of my father and what it must have been like for him.

One of the most evil and misguided men I have ever known, he never paid a day's consequence for his misdeeds, although it didn't prevent him from suffering intensely at the end. Though never publicly exposed, I knew that he had still paid for his crimes. A lifetime of regrets being an awful thing to take with you to the other side, my father was the epitome of someone who despaired in the end.

That night, I dreamed of a celebration—one of the most joyful dreams I've ever experienced. My past was complete and life was beginning anew, better than before. I was soon to find that no good deed goes unpunished, however, and as it turned out, I had still more to do in hell.

A FUNERAL AND A DEATH

My father's funeral gave my stepmother her moment to shine, although it was obvious that she did not understand the concept of "guilt by association." Posing as both victim and savior, she had the pastor refer to my father as a liar during his eulogy, and it got worse from there. Making the comment that he was "as much of a cheat in life as he was in cards," the pastor finished by saying that, while some might "consider him a piece of art," most just "considered him a piece of work."

It was not that the pastor was wrong, for my father was indeed all these things, what bothered me was that I knew the pastor was reading something my stepmother, his wife of thirty-six years, had written. As much as she would have liked to disassociate herself from him, she and my father were two peas in a pod— violent, vindictive, self-serving, manipulative pedophiles.

Dancing around like Rumpelstiltskin, she had the pastor talk about the plane my father used to have and how he flew back and forth between some "mines" they owned at the time in Dyre, Nevada. Knowing their past, I have always wondered what they may have left behind in those mines. I'll probably never know for sure, but at the time I found it strange how she talked about events that were so far in the past, as he hadn't flown since we left Omaha when I was a child.

Understanding later, I am thankful that she felt inclined to put this bit of info about my dad in his eulogy, as it reminded me of events in that plane I had done my best to forget like throwing children out at night to face certain death—a technique used to intimidate the rest of us because we were horrified that we'd be next. Shoving the past in our face was something she enjoyed, and she took the opportunity of my father's death to dance around triumphantly, believing she had won at last.

During the eulogy, I reached over and touched my sister Sarah's hand to calm her agitation at one point, whispering to her to cheer up because we were finally free of his terrible family. Just happy that Cindy wasn't there to witness our stepmother's circus, Tristan and I left before the last song ended due to my fantasies of punching the "bereaved" widow in the face.

I assumed, since my father was dead, that all the surprises were over and we were free. I couldn't have been more wrong, given our stepmother's obsessive need to taunt us with the skeletons our father assured us were in their closet.

Within days of his funeral, Cindy called from Florida and asked to come live with us, claiming she feared her husband and oldest daughter were planning to kill her. When she wouldn't tell us why they would do such a thing, I dismissed her insistence as just more of her penchant for drama. However, when she told her doctor and nurse about her fear, and they reported it to Adult Protective Services (APS), an investigation into her claims had just begun when she was found in her bedroom, dead at age fifty-four in Daytona, Florida.

Cindy:
dead @ 54

Due to her history of heart disease, no questions of foul play were asked, even though she'd been alone with her oldest daughter and husband the morning she died suspiciously (although I couldn't prove it).

I was devastated by Cindy's death. She as the oldest and I the youngest, and the fact that she was born on 6-12 and I was born on 12-6, bonded us in a strange way. It was true that we often fought like cats and dogs, but we also shared a special bond as siblings.

We had spoken for hours every day right after Dad died, leading right up to her death less than three weeks later, and I have always regretting not having taken her request for safe haven seriously. Soon after, when I became involved in an investigation regarding my family and their past activities, I would wonder what exactly she and Dad had discussed with regard to his skeletons in the closet. Eventually coming to believe that her death was connected to our past, she did, after all, remember everything that had transpired during our childhoods.

Again, I assumed the past was finally over. No more connections other than Sarah and her family, Tristan was incredibly grounding for me, although even he couldn't foresee what was coming. The ride was speeding up as, unable to leave well enough alone, my father's widow was just warming up.

LEST WE FORGET

Ten days after my father's death, I did a journey to help him cross to the other side (this was right before Cindy's death). As angry as I was with him, and as much as I despised his life and the things he was guilty of, I still loved him and couldn't leave him in the dark.

Praying for him throughout that time, I was hoping that he would have found his own way, but I found him in a place I had never been before. Though no lake of fire, I was wrong in my belief that there was no hell, for it was in this place that I found my father—naked, despairing, and alone. Huddled in the dark, two phantoms flew above his head, tormenting him. He was enveloped with guilt and shame. I looked into his vacant eyes and could see that he was trapped in a hell that he had constructed for himself, unaware of anything else.

I had no idea what to do, so I prayed for God's assistance. Before I had even finished my prayer, a gash developed in the darkness and two angels walked through it. Each took a side of my father and gently lifted him up and carried him into the light, disappearing instantly. I awakened and thanked God, the angels, and universe for helping to save my father.

My experience with Uriel had given me a new perspective. I realized that if God could forgive Uriel, whose crimes far exceeded my father's, and draw him back into heaven, I believed God would forgive my father. Taking it a step further, I discovered that if God could forgive, so could I. He was my father and it was my place to honor him, not judge him. Besides, considering the condition in which I found him, he seemed to be punishing himself enough for the two of us. All of life being energy, we all carry both the love we share and the evil we do to the other side, where we become our own judge, and he had obviously sentenced himself harshly.

Perhaps due to their own unorthodox pasts, neither my father nor stepmother appreciated my take on life and God. Sarah, researching info on the FBI's take on cults during her graduate studies, told me that members involved with satanic cults often become Jesus freaks when they break away, which certainly fit my father and stepmother.

As fundamentalist zealots, they used their religious convictions to condemn others while excusing themselves. Acting on the belief that Jesus only loves those they deemed acceptable, they told me that my sexuality was going to land me in hell, even though they were former practicing satanists, among their long list of crimes. Their hypocrisy was nauseating and often more than I could endure.

IT'S WHO YOU KNOW, NOT WHAT YOU KNOW

Although angry with my stepmother, I was not all that interested in taking her to court to fight for the blood money Sarah felt was owed us for our father's life insurance policies. Lawyers cost money and I didn't have any to spare for a legal battle. Sarah was furious that our father's widow had danced on his grave, but since she was as poor as we were, I figured the point was moot.

Then, magically, for some reason strings were pulled to "help us." Sarah had converted to Judaism at one point and thus was connected to the Jewish community in Omaha. Directing her to a prestigious law firm and a lawyer I'll call "Shady," her temple ended up suggesting we get legal counsel from him.

He turned out to be one of the sneakiest narcissists I have ever encountered. He disclosed that, although he also represented our stepmother's daughter's parents in law, who had married into a very rich and very prominent Jewish family in town, he

conflict of interest. Sarah assured me of his reputation even as he requested a $5,000 retainer.

Knowing that neither of us could come up with that kind of cash, Sarah and I were about to give up when a man by the name of Kevin Dobson offered to pony up the cash. Omaha's primary drug dealer during the 1980s, Dobson had been heavily involved with the coke trade from the Contras and was thus connected to many of the nefarious activities going on then.

He often bragged that he was connected to the whole Reagan/Bush Iran-Contra scandal, and he would detail how the Carter Lake/North Omaha chapter of Hell's Angels, along with the Omaha mafia, were able to smuggle kids and drugs out in the open. Considering that he was paralyzed from a wrestling injury in high school, I thought he was full of it and dismissed him as an idiot, even though I admitted to Sarah that I could see how someone could see him as being somewhat larger than life, even if it was in a malevolent, seedy kind of way.

Connected not only by the past but also through her husband's relationship with Kevin as his best friend, Sarah had a tumultuous relationship with the man. The man had done nothing but harm Sarah's relationships, yet, despite their history together, for some reason, he decided to write my sister a check out of nowhere, with the only condition that we use Shady and his law firm.

I told Sarah to decline his offer. Although I'd always discredited his stories, I was still wary that he might be connected to our past, but Sarah's husband pressured her into it, and not wanting her to have to go at it alone, I joined her. A month or so into the lawsuit to recover life insurance money, Sarah and I argued about the validity of Dobson's claims, so she forced me to Google his name, and what we found scared us both.

In reading the Omaha appeal concerning *United States of America v. Gilberto Montoya,* which had been submitted August 26, 1991, and decided December 26, 1991, we both discovered that Kevin had been telling the truth. Gilberto Montoya was Pablo Escobar's nephew, Pablo Escobar being the Contra cocaine dealer from Colombia whom the CIA had colluded with during the Iran-Contra scandal. Steven M. Watson argued for Montoya and Donald L. Schense for the U.S. government. I quote:

In June 1989, Florida residents Montoya and Juan Garcia-Escobar drove from Miami to Omaha with two kilograms of cocaine concealed in a cooler. They delivered it to their customer, Kevin Dobson, in the presence of Mike Dillon, Dobson's friend and a cocaine and marijuana user. Montoya and Garcia-Escobar remained in Omaha for several days until Dobson had sold enough of the cocaine to pay them for one kilo. They then returned to Miami where they were arrested some months later.

... Montoya was convicted of a conspiracy to distribute cocaine in Omaha in June 1989. The alleged conspirators were Montoya, Garcia-Escobar, and Dobson. Although the only transaction proved was the transporting from Florida and the distribution in Omaha of two kilos of cocaine in June 1989, the testimony tended to prove that the conspirators viewed this transaction as the start of a continuing relationship.

And they included an almost offhand comment by Dobson during his direct testimony:

Q. Mr. Dobson, what was that discussion in regards to fronting cocaine to you from Miami from Mr. Montoya and Juancho [Garcia-Escobar]?

A. *Juancho had told me that [Montoya] said that he would bring me up six kilos of cocaine and leave them with me, that I could sell it at my leisure along with a couple hundred pounds of pot ... for Mike Dillon to sell at his leisure.*

Dobson had always claimed that it was his information that had brought the Contra drug cartel down, and that his work with the CIA is what saved his ass. Faced with the irrefutable fact that he was telling the truth, it was reading those government papers that I began to realize that we just might be in over our heads. Just beginning to connect the dots, I began to wonder about the connection Kevin had with the people in our past, and why he was so adamant that Shady control our case?

HEALING AT LAST

My fortieth birthday on December 6, 2006, was a complete game changer for me. No longer plagued by nightmares or the fear that I was the Antichrist, my experience with Uriel, although overwhelming and strange, had healed many parts of me long needing it. I had come to consider the experience as one where my mind had simply repaired itself rather than some strange spiritual experience, and had succeeded in lulling myself into a false sense of security.

The day before my birthday was uneventful. But that night I kept waking up in a panic. Unable to recall my dreams, it was on awakening for the fifth time that night that I realized something unconscious was on the move. Closing my eyes, I went back to sleep with the intention of waking up in the dream so I could see what I was so afraid to face.

I found myself standing in the middle of a pentagram with twelve people standing around me in a circle, chanting. In the dream, unable to ascertain why Uriel hadn't taken me over yet, the group of them had decided to perform a ceremony in order to coax my soul out of my body long enough for Uriel to take control. Desperate to regain the control they'd lost, I realized they were obviously oblivious of Uriel's crossing the March before.

Being in the middle of a pentagram as a child had been familiar territory, but being psychologically forced back into it as an adult raised an instant and consuming rage, and I demanded that they stop what they were doing immediately. Waking up, in so many more ways than one, I opened my eyes and got out of bed.

I looked at the clock and saw that it was six in the morning, and I suddenly became resolved as to what I had to do. Most people would have just assumed it was a dream and let it go, but I awoke that morning knowing that what had just transpired was real. No longer convinced that my experience with Uriel was imagined, I decided to go on a journey to find him and see what was happening on the other side.

I decided to ask my therapist Dr. Smith to help with my perceived task, as I was unsure just exactly who the group was in my dream and didn't want to take any chances, believing I was battling spiritual warfare. There was no part of me that doubted what had just happened, and the thought that I was still spiritually connected to those who had practiced Satanism during my childhood was unnerving.

I believed in the magic these people like to wield, and the child part of me was scared, so I asked Dr. Smith, as a fellow shaman, for help to insure a safe journey.

Always having adhered to the philosophy of "two or three gathered in My Name," I knew that having another person drum and sing prayers of protection was more powerful than doing the journey alone. Able to offer prayers for guidance and protection, the drumming shaman effectively watches over the one journeying, and as my therapist and someone who understands my spiritual practice, I felt Dr. Smith was my best bet.

In her office, after I told her about my dream about the pentagram and what had happened, Dr. Smith agreed to help, so she lit a candle while offering a prayer for protection. Quietly beating her drum, I went into my trance, and as the wavelengths of my brain began changing from beta to delta, I proceeded inside and began to dream.

I found Uriel alone. He was surrounded by darkness, almost like that place I found my father. Realizing that things had not gone quite as I'd hoped during the extractment, Uriel had become entangled by the bonds of his own making, which trapped him in some sort of limbo or *bardo*, caught between the middle world and the other side.

Somehow waking that morning intuitively knowing what I had to do, I proceeded to ask him if he would release those who had been sacrificed to him. Asking him had an immediate and intense effect, and what transpired next was one of the most beautiful things I have ever seen on the other side. The experience profoundly changed me forever.

The darkness surrounding Uriel disappeared instantly. It was replaced with a blinding light that exploded from within him, so intense I was forced to look away. Materializing out of thin air, three gigantic ornate gates appeared before me and began opening. Behind the gates, I could see the shoreline of a new world not far away, and it dawned on me that I was witnessing the gates of the amazingly beautiful new Earth opening.

I then noticed a countless number of souls, all of whom had been released from their sacrificial bondage to Uriel, migrating in droves toward the gates. Awakened from a deep slumber, they were singing and celebrating a return to life. The experience was breathtaking.

The sheer numbers of souls told me that Uriel had been on the rampage far longer than I'd realized, and all of heaven seemed to be celebrating Uriel's release. Uriel was now bathed in light, his chains dissipating as he spread his wings and stretched off the last of the darkness.

The high-pitched melodies of the songs I was hearing in my journey had begun to physically affect Dr. Smith's drum, and the combination of the two was exquisite. Right before I ended my journey, I visualized the pentagram from my previous night's dream in the palm of my hand. I symbolically equated it with the coven's power, then blew into my palm and scattered the pentagram like sands to the wind.

I thanked Uriel, who was beaming. It was the first time I'd ever seen him smile, and I felt his love wash over me as I returned to myself.

Dr. Smith clamored to know what had happened, remarking that her drum had never sounded so beautiful or powerful, and after I told her what I had experienced, she asked what I made of it all. Stating with certitude that humankind was on the verge of a spiritual awakening, whether the prophesized "last days" or not, and although I didn't yet understand the ramifications, I assured her that something big had occurred.

A pragmatist, I think Dr. Smith was unsure what to make of what I told her, but even more at a loss, when two weeks later, the Republican Party fell apart in such a way that you needed a scorecard to keep up with the scandals hitting the media. Although I am not trying to suggest that all Republicans are satanists, as such an assertion would be silly, I do believe the material and spiritual worlds influence each other in their attempt to reach a balance of energies.

Changed by what I had just experienced in my journey in ways I had yet to comprehend, I decided that it was time to explore my family's past in order to validate childhood experiences I was now remembering. From this point on, things were going to get very, very strange.

13

DOWN THE
RABBIT HOLE

I t was after my fortieth birthday in 2006 that I began being inundated with memories. I kept dreaming of the little girl whose father my family murdered when I was ten, so I decided to see if I could find any information about them, but had no idea where to even start.

Sarah suggested I start with the National Center for Missing and Exploited Children website to see if I could pull up any files on missing children in the Omaha area, but I discovered that the files only went to 1984, and I was researching cases in the 1970s, so I hit a brick wall.

I called the center to ask for advice and spoke with a woman who, having no viable suggestions, still offered to file a verbal report and send it to the proper authorities. Figuring there was nothing to lose, I told her all the details I could remember, even those that had come through nightmares, expecting that would be the end of it when I hung up the phone.

In January 2007, I received a phone call from a Nebraska State Patrol officer. Incredibly polite, he explained that he wanted to ask me about some of the details in my verbal report, while giving me the impression that he might have something he hoped to flesh out.

Only once did he become agitated with me, and that was when he asked me why I hadn't called the police myself years earlier. I explained that I didn't think anyone would believe me. He demanded to know if I thought what I remembered was "real or not," and his demeanor further indicated to me that he knew something he wasn't revealing.

After assuring him that what I remembered did in fact happen, he then told me he'd be in touch if he needed any more information.

For the first time in my life, I had hope that something in my past might be substantiated, and I began trying to figure out what I could do to help, but after waiting two weeks and hearing nothing, I called the Nebraska State Patrol back and spoke with the officer in charge of cold cases.

I explained that I had filed a report with the National Center for Missing and Exploited Children and had received a phone call from an officer whose name I didn't remember. I wanted to find out who he was so I could speak with him. After getting the gist of it, the officer said he would be in contact as soon as he discovered anything.

Another week went by with nothing, so I decided to contact a local KETV reporter Brian Mastre who had just done a story on one of the abducted children, Todd Bequette, back in the 1970s. I met him at a local coffee shop and paraphrased my story, including the report I'd filed and my conversations with the officers.

Before we parted, he asked if I had any objection with his contacting the Nebraska State Patrol. Unlike the police, he actually called me back the next day, telling me that the Nebraska State Patrol had no evidence that I had even lived in Fremont, Nebraska, the small town near Omaha where the crime was committed. Frustrated and confused, I called my old elementary school and had them fax my school records to both the reporter and me.

I became concerned that I seemed to be facing another cover-up at the hands of Omaha's finest, so I decided to jump in with both feet and immerse myself in my own investigation. Determined, I bought a video camera and began recording videos detailing my situation and uploading them on YouTube, trying to make sense of it.

I filmed the first video outside my family's duplex in Fremont, where, in the basement, I was forced to light a man on fire. I implored the public to come forth with any information they might have, and I posted both the Nebraska State Patrol cold case officer's contact number as well as the reporter's.

When I told our lawyer about my first conversation with the Nebraska State Patrol and briefly described the original crime, Shady was uneasy but assured me that if it came to dropping the insurance recovery case against my stepmother in favor of a criminal investigation, he'd definitely allow it. I figured that a criminal case took precedence over a civil case, and I didn't want anything to jeopardize any investigation, to which he agreed, wishing me luck.

Sarah was beside herself with what I was attempting to do, not because of our impending court case against our stepmother but because she'd concluded a long time ago that there was nothing we could do to achieve any justice for what had happened to us and now wanted only to forget and move on. She urged me to stay out of it, warning me that there would only be heartache and no one would listen.

In retrospect, I probably should have listened to her because, in the end, she was right, but at the time, however, I believed that exposing the crimes my father was guilty of was my duty as his son. I believe in generational karma and, as such, have always felt that the sins of the father fell upon the shoulders of the son. Knowing what I knew and my place in all of it being what it was, I felt that I had to at least try.

Dr. Smith, although she understood my reasoning, also had concerns, but she explained once again that it wasn't her place to take sides. She admitted that she didn't know much about what I was speaking about, so we spent our sessions trying to help me focus on coming to terms with the grief I felt over losing three family members in such close succession (my dad, my sister Cindy, and my brother, Stephen).

The second ten-minute video I filmed was more detailed than the first, and I wrote it to better detail my postings on the Internet and to give Dr. Smith a better idea of what I was up against. In an attempt to explore my past and the implications of my experiences, I wrote the following speech that started things spinning so fast that, in the end, not even Dr. Smith would be able to prevent me from becoming the beaten and broken man I would become within the next year and a half.

My drama started with this speech, which I had entitled, "You Need to Know Why I Still Need Help in Solving a Murder." It attracted every nut case involved with my past, so here is the transcript of that video.

I did a previous video entitled "I Need Help in Solving a Murder" in which I am seeking any information I can find on a man who went missing in 1976 or so after going in search of his missing daughter—a man, most likely a policeman, my family

forced me to kill. It is difficult to explain the compli
situation in which I find myself, let alone in a ten-minute vi...
and I have never liked being in front of the camera, so added to
the intensity of where I was and what I was saying, needless to
say I was nervous. Hopefully, this will be better, although after I
am finished, there are those who are going to think that I'm nuts.
Funny enough, I've been where you are, and that was exactly my
mindset at the time. However, things change, and now for me it
has become a question of whether or not I will do what I believe
is the right thing, regardless of the consequences. After a lot of
soul searching, I know unequivocally that there are times when
one must stand alone if need be to do what he knows is right.
Some things must be defended, especially those who cannot defend
themselves, regardless of the cost. So with that, I want to explain
why I think I have had to go to such extraordinary lengths to get
a murder investigated.

As outlandish as this may sound, the real story behind the
Franklin Credit Union, the biggest scandal ever to hit Omaha, was
that in the 1960s and the 1970s, George H.W. Bush, Sr., head of the
CIA during part of that time, was conducting secret experiments
on the effects of extreme torture and fear on children in a funeral
home in North Omaha—just one of the things happening to
children disappearing during a rash of child abductions here in
Omaha in the 1970s, abductions that are well known and yet have
never been investigated, let alone prosecuted. I believe this is what
prosecuting attorney Gary Caradori discovered when he and his
eight-year-old son AJ were blown out of the sky. Funny enough,
after his death, all of the investigations into what was happening
in Omaha stopped abruptly.

It has been hard for me to accept that the very year I try to have this crime investigated, one hundred police officers, an unprecedented number for Omaha and unfortunately the very people who could help, all suddenly retire. Two weeks before the police chief himself abruptly retired, President Bush himself was in town. I cannot help but feel that all of this is because they realize the same thing I do: that although hundreds of reports police received regarding children being abused have disappeared, chances are the victims who made those reports haven't. And neither are they now children.

Chances are, people out there still remember the big white funeral home decorated in over-the-top Victorian décor, every room a parlor. They may even remember the closets leading to passageways and the terrible hide-and-seek game in which if you were found you were killed. The passageways were tunnels from so dark you couldn't see to so bright you were blinded. Children had a hard time thinking because they were so drugged and terrified of the screams of children being tortured somewhere beyond where they were hiding. Hummel Park

Perhaps some people remember the gatherings in Hummel Park where child after child was raped on the grand staircase. Or how the entrances to the north side of the park were blocked and the so-called Devil's Head was not so much a talisman as it was a lookout point on which you could see the traffic for miles in both directions. Maybe they remember the scary band of drunken, drugged pedophiles and their cult-like behavior.

I remember recurring nightmares that I believed could simply not be real. But I'll bet this is a recurring theme in documents that no longer exist, especially considering the people I've spoken to

who have had the same recurring nightmares. How is this even possible unless it is not a nightmare but a series of memories?

With as many problems as George W. Bush has in his presidency, to imagine that he wouldn't be concerned with a situation that could shift the debate of whether the Bush Administration tortures people to exactly how long he and his family have been practicing the art, and exactly who they have tortured before we had camps around the world, seems unlikely. Neither Sr. nor Jr. was born president; they were born like the rest of us, so to speak, and therefore are subject to the laws of man, just like the rest of us, whether or not they ended up in positions of power. And though this may surprise them, they are definitely subject to the laws of God.

And to those who consider me a conspiracy theorist, let me ask you a question. Had I come to you ten years ago and told you that the Catholic Church would be almost bankrupt due to a conspiracy to protect, hide, and reroute hundreds of pedophile priests, what would you have said? More importantly, what do you know now? Interestingly enough, I have discovered that the Catholic Church was involved in Omaha, too, and allowed Boys Town orphans to be used by pedophiles not limited to Catholic priests.

The abduction of Todd Bequette is only one case illustrating the blatant absence of investigations into abductions in the 1970s. Todd was abducted at age thirteen in the Old Market, a hunting ground for children at the time. Now an adult, Todd hasn't been able to get anything about his case, no paperwork of any kind, nothing about how the police did nothing, or about Terry Roy Holman never being prosecuted or even charged in Nebraska, or about how private detective Denny Whelan finally found him. It is as though he was never abducted. Todd and I have emailed a few times and he has told me that he does not believe his case has *anything to do with the Franklin Credit Union. I believe he is right, but I have a feeling he and the children he was forced to lure have everything to do with the case I am speaking about. If nothing else, the Todd Bequette case is a big shiny red flag leaving me with the question of why—if so many children were being abducted at the time—why was there never any investigations into them, let alone prosecutions?*

If the city of Omaha can afford to give such extravagant retirements to their police force, then surely they can afford investigations into such heinous accusations, especially considering how many accusations have been made. And to those Omaha officers receiving such generous pensions: surely you realize that this is unfinished business that happened on your watch, and that it is totally unfair to ask the citizens of Omaha to pay so handsomely for a job that wasn't done; and surely, in all the decades these allegations have been there to pursue, there was ample time to do thorough investigations. Alisha Owen was sent to prison for years after making allegations, so there must be some paperwork that can show what did and did not happen in Omaha involving child abductions and abuse. Whatever the case, I am sure that Omaha's finest will rise to the challenge and do what must be done. After all, for Omaha PD to not protect our children and to not prosecute those who abuse them is a major dereliction of duties and not the legacy anyone honorable would wish to leave.

I believe we as a society must stop this double standard of justice. Our leaders must be held accountable for their actions just as we the people they serve are held accountable for ours. What happened to me at ten has been called the rite of accountability, meaning you are forced to do a crime and can't talk. Otherwise, you'd be held accountable and go to jail. This is the rub. Now as an adult, I am doing this because I am holding myself accountable, and because I believe it's the right thing to do. I will not stop.

So Fred, <u>dear friend of Alan B</u>aer of thirty-five years, it makes no difference how many death threats you send my way. I will not stop until I find healing and closure for those who have been hurt by this mess. I feel an obligation to do this. It is like I said in the card I sent you: do not let old age overcome you before you make this right because if you do, I fear the consequences of your behavior will be dire. As a man of God, you should realize that in the end God will not be denied. Your behavior pains me because I considered you a very dear friend. But judging by your threats, you are not only involved but have something to hide as well.

Hopefully, my next step is to set up a contest. If the police won't look into this, perhaps amateur investigators would like to try. One way or another, it will be looked at. We live in a different day and age; secrets are not as easily kept as they once were. And these allegations are far from new. What IS new is that they are being made by someone whose family was intimately connected. As strange is it may sound, I believe we are at a turning point in society, and to fight for the darkness is to be owned by the darkness. Like it or not, at one point or another, every one of us is going to face God.

I can't tell you who to call; I wish I knew myself. Maybe just send out the word and we can reach some point of closure in this together as a people. Funny enough, I really feel like God is with me in this, so any prayers you could offer that these people find closure, healing, and peace would be great. Thanks again—and I will most likely be seeing you later. Peace.

THE WONDERLAND POLKA

Hell's Angel [handwritten note]

Within two months after posting the video, I was contacted by a woman on YouTube connected with a website devoted to the Franklin Credit Union and all of the conspiracies surrounding the failed bank. She said her father had been a Hell's Angel murdered on an Indian reservation, and she had many tales of government conspiracies that included black helicopters targeting her house and phone lines.

After researching her story and discovering that there was some truth to what she was saying, I decided not to dismiss her. Considering what I was posting, I figured it was best not to judge and so I decided to check out the website she suggested. *franklinfiles* (franklinfiles.net) was filled with information that was posted onto a forum and also contained a chat area that encouraged survivors to communicate with each other. The forum introduced me to the nuances of the Franklin Credit Union case, and it was on *franklinfiles* that I first saw Michael Aquino, an event that would bring my world crashing down.

I learned through the interaction of the postings about the existence of MK-ULTRA's mind-control experiments and its connections to the Franklin scandal, and I discovered a plethora of leads, while at the same time, I realized with dismay that I wouldn't be able to do any kind of meaningful investigation.

I still suffered from PTSD, and the effect that *franklinfiles* had on me is hard to explain, even now. But I realized that all of the craziness of my past was not only possible but probable, and I would later come to see myself as some strange version of the fictional Jason Bourne character who was searching for his past.

Everything I had been taught as a child started to, for the first time ever, make sense.

Watching Michael Aquino in videos on the talk show circuit, I saw the man in my dreams parade around in his Merlin outfits, and discovered how connected he still was to things I had told myself couldn't exist. I was no longer able to placate myself by telling myself that I was crazy.

Needless to say, the website triggered me. Coming so close to my past fed the paranoia I already felt on a daily basis, and I started to become irritated that I couldn't get anyone to listen considering there was so much evidence to back me up. At the same time, I was angry that I had to go to such extremes as shooting videos and calling police to have my past investigated.

In the beginning, *franklinfiles* was an outlet for me, which allowed me to express myself and help to relieve some of the stress. Posts on *franklinfiles* encouraged me to talk about my experiences and offered their support as I began relating memories of my past to complete strangers. I believed that the truth would somehow set me free.

The more I read about all the issues tangential to the Franklin Credit Union, the less it all made sense. That was until I discovered the Johnny Gosch case. Gosch was a paperboy who disappeared in 1982 in Des Moines, Iowa (one of several actually, supposedly with no connections to the paperboys who also disappeared in Omaha, not counting the two for which John Joubert was executed for). His mother had written a book entitled *Why Johnny Can't Come Home* (2000) detailing before and after events, and *franklinfiles* was aggressively dedicated to her quest.

> Joubert Dies for Boys' Murders: Last of Appeals Rejected Hours Before Execution, July 17, 1996, *Omaha World-Herald* (p. 1): John Joubert was electrocuted at 12:14 a.m. today for the murders of two Sarpy County boys.

The Gosch case started to make me question everything in a new way. First, police had refused to investigate his disappearance from the very beginning. They claimed he was a runaway, despite the fact that he wasn't the only paperboy who had disappeared in the Des Moines area. Second, and probably more important to me at the time, Michael Aquino, the U.S. Army lieutenant colonel who is also the founder of well-known Satanic church Temple of Set, was said to be connected to this case, according to Johnny's mother Noreen Gosch.

Knowing that this man had been involved in (1) MK-ULTRA, (2) the Presidio day care "satanic panic" scandal, and (3) was personally involved with the Bush family, I began to think I might have to battle my nightmare man in real life.

I was taught as a child that if you control the perception of a thing, you control the thing itself; therefore, I began to see a pattern with concerns to those most well-known with the controversial events in Omaha. Take Aquino, for example. A long career in the psych ops department of the military, with strong enough convictions in Satanism that he founded Temple of Set, along with his sordid history that could logically connect him with the nation's satanic panic experienced decades before, he seems to have surrounded himself with

Hummel Park

people who accused him, not of ritualistically abusing children to commune with demons, but rather of being involved with aliens and alien abductions.

He bounced between touting his prestigious military career to defending himself from inane accusations. Even today, he promotes a victim-like quality about himself, encouraging people to focus on those who persecute him rather than on Aquino himself.

I continued making videos detailing what I'd gone through and posted a longer video on MySpace detailing the events that had happened in a densely wooded area of Omaha called Hummel Park, which is isolated on the far edge of town, where many of the child sacrifices occurred.

The main entrance to Omaha's Hummel Park.

The pentagram inlaid in stone on the pavilion floor.

Inside the pavilion at
Hummel Park and one of two
massive stone fireplaces.

Approach to the pavilion
in Hummel Park.

The grand stone staircase in Hummel Park.

The outlook and vista from Hummel Park
where watchers stood guard.

Human sacrifices were taking place in the park's open-air pavilion while children were being raped on the stone steps several hundred feet down a hill from the pavilion. Guards stood watch at all park entrances so no one could get in (or out). Interestingly, a five-pointed star is inlaid in stone on the floor of the pavilion.

> "The pentagram, or five-pointed star, has long been a symbol used by various people who practice ritual magic. ... It may either signify the Order of the Eastern Star, a Masonic women's auxiliary organization, or modern Satanism" (Noblitt and Perskin, p. 145).

Dr. Smith spent hours listening to me relate what I was experiencing in my life, as well as what was happening on *franklinfiles*. She was growing more and more concerned that I was getting involved with strangers whose intentions were unknown. I spent hours at the computer in a chat room becoming addicted to learning as much as I could about child abuse and abductions in Omaha.

Much of what I was hearing made no sense compared to what I knew to be true, and, verbalizing my befuddlement, I began to see the attitudes in the chat room change. Tristan was right. This was a complete waste of time. Internet "relationships" were as manipulative and undependable as my family's mix of truth and lies.

People on *franklinfiles* encouraged me to contact a retired FBI agent by the name of Ted Gunderson (he died in 2011). He said he had taken over the investigation into Franklin Credit Union allegations after Gary Caradori was killed in the plane crash. One of the first things he told me was that the CIA and government were infested with satanists who had attacked him with a

<u>microwave weapon.</u> Even though he came off as a lunatic, Ted was nonetheless a <u>wealth of information, so I befriended him.</u>

RAY GUNS? REALLY?

Nonlethal microwave weapons, much like the sci-fi "ray gun," direct energy that can cause burning and pain and can be used for crowd control or to disable vehicles. Also called Active Denial Systems, these weapons are being developed by the U.S. military. Credible sources such as *The Boston Globe* (Ray gun, sci-fi staple, meets reality, September 24, 2004) and the BBC are reporting on the testing.

"The Active Denial System is a non-lethal weapon designed to disperse violent crowds and repel enemies," according to Dan Cairns reporting for the BBC (July 15, 2010). "It uses a focused invisible beam that causes an 'intolerable heating sensation,' but only penetrates the skin to the equivalent of three sheets of paper."

The Finders

Agent Gunderson sent me a document entitled <u>*The Finders Report*</u> he'd written <u>detailing activities of a CIA-sponsored child abduction group known as The Finders. In it,</u> I was introduced <u>to the scope of what my family had been involved with.</u> Ted's <u>assertion of a large, secret, and protected group of men who were networking to abduct children</u> for a variety of purposes, from <u>MK-ULTRA</u> to <u>satanic sacrifices, and making an inordinate</u> amount of money from their activities, was believable.

THE FINDERS

"CIA Front established in the 1960's It has TOP CLEARANCE and PROTECTION in its ASSIGNED task of kidnapping and torture-programming young children throughout the U.S. Members are specially trained GOVERNMENT KIDNAPPERS known to be sexual degenerates who involve the kidnapped children in Satanic sex orgies and bloody rituals as well as murders of other children and slaughter of animals. They use a fleet of unmarked vans to grab TARGETED children from parks and schoolyards. In doing so they use children within their organization as decoys to attract the victims close to the vans where they are grabbed by the adults. They then drug the children and transport them to a series of safe houses for safe keeping. They are then used in their ceremonies for body parts, sex slaves and some are auctioned off at various locations in the northern hemisphere." Transcribed from a handwritten note on letterhead identified as Ted L. Gunderson and Associates, Santa Monica, California. Gunderson is identified on the letterhead as Member, Society of Former Special Agents of the Federal Bureau of Investigation (obtained from *The Finders Report* supplied to the author by Gunderson, no date)

McMartin Pre-School Investigator May Probe Abuse in Nebraska, May 24, 1991, *Omaha World-Herald* (p. 14): A retired FBI agent who made headlines investigating child abuse allegedly connected with a Southern California preschool said Thursday night that he may be asked to launch an investigation of child abuse in Nebraska. Ted Gunderson said he flew to Nebraska Thursday morning at the request of the Nebraska Leadership Conference, a group that contends that child abuse and ritualistic cult activity are growing problems in the Cornhusker State. ... Gunderson attracted national attention last year when he said evidence of child abuse had been detected in tunnels and a secret room allegedly uncovered beneath the McMartin Pre-School in Manhattan Beach, Calif.

Group Hires Former FBI Agent to Assist in Child-Abuse Probe, June 3, 1991, *Omaha World-Herald* (p. 11).

Retired Agent Warns of Satanism; Critic Says Claims Not Credible, August 18, 1991, *Omaha World-Herald* (p. 10B): A Lincoln businessman says he is convinced that a retired FBI agent will provide that Nebraska children have been kidnapped and murdered. "He's made some startling discoveries in national cases," Ed Weaver Jr. of Lincoln said of former FBI agent Ted Gunderson, who says he plans to oversee an investigation in Nebraska this fall. ... "There is a satanic cult movement in this country," Gunderson said. "It is active, and they have virtually infiltrated every level of society, including law enforcement." ... "My adversaries, in most instances, are satanists," Gunderson said. "Also, there are a lot of people who are just plain ignorant about it."

In reviewing the Justice Department figures concerning child disappearances on the National Center for Missing and Exploited Children website, it was evident to me that something was devouring our nation's children in the shadows.

Unfortunately, very few connected to the mess in Omaha seemed to be who they presented themselves to be, and people on *franklinfiles* found my concerns to be unpopular. I was eventually banned from interacting on the website.

People who had expressed a desire to help me now began threatening and ridiculing me, and I had no way to respond. Later, I would hear *franklinfiles* referred to as a "sponge site," which was designed to bring survivors forward, befriend them, and encourage them to talk, until reaching a certain point, at which time these unidentified people on the websites turn on the survivors and do their best to discredit them.

Feeling angry and discredited, I redoubled my efforts and recorded another video for YouTube and entitled it, "A Walking Tour through Pedophile Heaven—Omaha, Nebraska's Real Legacy." I filmed a thirty-minute walk through the Old Market area, up to the police station, and then over to The Run, I point out many of the places that were connected with the Franklin Credit allegations of child prostitution and abuse and showed how close in proximity everything was while demonstrating that there was no way that Robert Wadman and the local police department were unaware of what was taking place in town. I called for a complete reinvestigation.

I decided it was time to finally confront the publicly involved personalities, like former police chief Robert Wadman and Michael Aquino. Feeling as if I had been inducted into a war, I was willing to put myself on the front lines.

I confronted Robert Wadman first, and following is a series of emails I had with him in June 2008. [Note: There is a one-hour time zone difference.]

< 06/24/2008 6:12 am >

Robert,

I was very disappointed not to hear anything from you after sending you an email, so I thought I would try again. You see, my friend, I have tried to get my parents to take me to court about all of this over and over and over to no avail, so when I was told that you were eager to take people to court, I figured we could help each other out. I am willing to bet that I can help to make this happen, so let's just say that both of us have had a prayer answered.

I just wanted to let you know that the videos are definitely NOT the only thing I am guilty of doing. The communications I have had with the media, politicians, and victim advocacy groups have almost been daily, and now that I am involved with this to such a degree, it has pretty much taken over my life. You see, this time I know you don't have the Alan and Marsha Baer foundation money to think about since he's dead and out of the picture. So now, maybe we can get some real discourse about all of this. I mean, did you really think it was fair to send Mark Andersen, one of my dearest friends, and Walt Carlson, the man you all dubbed "The Pied Piper of Porn," to jail for years while not even giving so much as a slap on the hand to Alan and his sex with minors counts?

I have also sent everyone on a similar mission. You see, if they start looking at all that child porn being collected in Europe, we all know that they are not only going to see the eatery Stars (down in the Old Market) but especially in the child porn and snuff films they'll see The Hollywood—you know, the one Omaha tore down when all of these allegations came out. I'll bet you weren't betting on anyone remembering any of this. Funny how Ted Gunderson and his friends didn't know anything about it.

Last of all and probably most importantly, I've told people that the bodies of those children are buried in legitimate graves in Forest Lawn Memorial Park off of 48th Street in North Omaha. I know you guys thought you were so clever about that, but let me ask you this (now that people know about it and are looking into it): exactly HOW are you going to retrieve what you left? IF you don't, you realize you're leaving it open for someone else to go and look. And I assure you, everyone is going to want to see.

This is the deal, Robbie: you all better deal with this before you draw your last breath because if you don't, you're going to end up right along with your savior and friend Alan Baer, who, by the way, won't be saving anyone's ass this time. Get your fancy clothes ready because one way or another, we are going to end up in court. Noreen Gosch is the LEAST OF YOUR WORRIES NOW, MY FRIEND. By the way, you attack her one more time and I'll return the favor. You do have media where you live, don't you? So far, everyone has been really, really interested in this, so I bet the people in your hometown would find it equally so. Better call your lawyer now.

You want to deal with someone, threaten someone, or intimidate someone—well, here I am, Robbie. I'm listed, feel free to call. Just realize that I will be recording the call and sharing it with everyone when we are done. Things aren't going to go well for all of you with all of this, FRIEND.

I look forward to hearing from you. (xxx) xxx-xxxx.

P.S.

Also, Noreen Gosch—you remember, the mother you've been intimidating and harassing for trying to get answers for 25 years now about her abducted son—has nothing to do with this. I am cc'ing her so she can see what I am doing. After I send this, I'll be sending it out to everyone else, but I don't feel you need to know who they are. That will be your surprise.

----- Original Message ----

From: Robert WADMAN

To: d shur

Sent: Wednesday, June 25, 2008 10:55:26 AM

Subject: Re: Hey Robbie- its your old friend from Omaha again

Mr. D. Shur:

I'm sure you are aware that Alisha Owen was found guilty of perjury for the lies she told about Robert Wadman. These same lies are now being spread by Noreen Gosch. If she doesn't want to be sued, all she has to do is delete the lies about Robert Wadman from her web-site. She is a sad case, and the only reason she has not been sued is her pathetic position. Robert Wadman had nothing to do with any of the things she has experienced. If her lies are not removed, she will be filed against. Just ask yourself, why would she put my phone number and e-mail address on her web-page? If she

wants nothing to do with this situation, all she has to do is stop spreading lies about me.

Dr. Robert Wadman

Professor

Criminal Justice Department

>>> d shur < 6/25/2008 9:59 AM >>>

Robert-

We are not speaking of Noreen. What I would like is for you to respond to my accusations. You realize that they only need to find one child in those graves to credit what I am saying. Whether or not Noreen Gosch is sad is beside the point. But since this was all going on and you were chief of police at the time, are you actually going to tell me that you have no idea what I am talking about? Really?

I'll bet I can prove otherwise or at least give it some help. By the way, when I told her that Sam was my boss and manager at The Stage Door, she was incredibly thankful. So you really think I am the only gay man left alive that remembers that? Really?

I look forward to hearing from you. And more than that, I hope that we can eventually meet in person because I would love to have people interview the two of us together. Doesn't that sound like fun?

D

From: Robert WADMAN
To: d shur
Sent: Wednesday, June 25, 2008 11:13:17 AM
D
My phone number is (xxx)xxx-xxxx. I'm at my office and I would be glad to talk to you about the nonsense you are writing about. I have never been involved with any of the allegations you are making. Your writing appears to be a little nutty and I want you to know Directly from me how hurtful these lies have been to me and my family.
Dr. Robert Wadman

---

d shur < 6/25/2008 10:18 AM >>>
Robert,
I'll call this afternoon. I need to set some things up, but then I would be more than glad to talk with you. If you have never heard of any of these allegations, then how exactly have they hurt you? Neither Noreen nor most people know what I am talking about, so I have been very solid on sending out daily emails explaining all of this. I know: you all thought that if anyone would say anything about this they would sound nuts. But you know, I was told you were this evil big bad man who attacked at a moment's notice and your emails sound as if you are shaken. I bet I can help increase that.
I'll be talking to you this afternoon.
Look forward to it,
D

From: Robert WADMAN

To: d shur

Sent: Wednesday, June 25, 2008 11:23:21 AM

D:

I won't be in my office this afternoon and you don't need to set anything up. I have been hurt because the lies about me have destroyed my consulting business.

Have a little courage and give me a call.

Dr. Wadman

----

d shur < 6/25/2008 10:25 AM >>>

Trust me, Robert, I have courage. But I also know that you are a game player. That's okay. I come from a family of game players. I am just not home right now. But trust me, I will be calling you. Have no doubt about that.

D

From: Robert WADMAN

To: d shur

Sent: Wednesday, June 25, 2008 11:30:07 AM

D:

It is obvious that you don't have enough common sense to just call. Are living in a fantasy world with no real people in your life. Call (xxx) xxx-xxxx. I would be glad to answer any of your questions. If you don't have the courage to call, stop bothering me.

Robert Wadman

d shur > 6/25/2008 10:39 AM >>>
It is DEFINITELY not going to be that easy. We both know that I am not going anywhere, nor are all the people that I have told. Hmmmm. Babyland. Does this area in Forest Lawn sound familiar? Big joke, huh? Let's see if you keep laughing.
D.

From: Robert WADMAN
To: d shur
Sent: Wednesday, June 25, 2008 11:44:08 AM
Even though you [sic] statements appear to be idiotic, I would be glad to talk with you at anytime. I have a search firm looking up your address and I will be in touch.
Robert Wadman

---

d shur < 6/25/2008 10:53 AM >>>
Robert-
We both know that you are desperate to find out what I know. The problem for you is not what I know, but what I have told. I am not just some kid who found himself in this. I grew up with it. I know so much more than you are comfortable with.

I have told about everything, friend. Babyland means something to you, as it should.

Funny- you don't seem to be full of threats with me. And calling me crazy might work with someone who isn't self-aware, but we all know you are fucked. This is all coming out, and as police chief, especially with your history concerning all of this, I don't think you are going to be able to separate yourself.

I will be calling you today.

D

From: Robert WADMAN
To: d shur
Sent: Wednesday, June 25, 2008 12:42:46 PM
D:

I've tracked from www.xxxxxxxxx.com/world/murderous-secret-need-be-uncovered-Omaha. They referred me to "GoDaddy.com" which is apparently your web-master. Give me a little more time, and you will be in contact with my attorney.

Robert Wadman

>>> d shur < 6/25/2008 11:51 AM >>>

You know, it occurred to me that you have my phone number as well. As far as your attorney, send the paperwork because I ain't gonna stop until we are in court. But I think I made that quite clear in my email – you know, the one you read on [other web postings] and myspace, and Noreen put it on her site at my request and won't take it down until I AM TOLD BY A JUDGE to remove it.

I am not afraid of you, dude. I know who I am. You do, too, I think. Karma can be a real bitch.

D.

----- Original Message ----

From: Robert WADMAN

To: d shur

Sent: Wednesday, June 25, 2008 12:54:59 PM

D:

I know you are in Council Bluffs and there are four different Shur in the area. I'm trying to get it narrowed down.

Robert Wadman

>>> d shur < 6/25/2008 12:07 PM >>>

Robert,

You have my phone number. Call the Nebraska state patrol guy, I'm sure he will help you.

Of course, I already have given everyone all of your shit, and emailed all of this correspondence to everyone.

You, my friend, are going to deal with me, and not the way you think, either. And if anything should happen to me, I have given everyone enough info to go ahead, as well as made hours of video tapes talking about it all. You do know that the Supreme Court has ruled that type of info can be used in a trial?

We live in a different day and age, dude. Do what you want and I'll make sure I bring it right to your front step.

D

----- *Original Message* ----

From: Robert WADMAN

To: d shur

Sent: Wednesday, June 25, 2008 1:18:14 PM

D:

I've tried (xxx) xxx-xxxx. Is this the right number?

Robert Wadman

Robert,

Oh boy, now I can show that you got hold of my stepmother who has been dealing with this for about a year and a half now. She left me a message on my YouTube videos. I am sure you old friends have quite a bit to talk about, you and my dad being in the same child-killing cult.

Thanks. That's what I was looking for.

D

P.S.

By the way, my phone number is (xxx) xxx-xxxx, as I PLAINLY TOLD YOU IN MY EMAIL.

By the way, she already knows I'm not afraid of her. Maybe you should try calling your friend Alan. Oh wait, he can't help you.

Forest Lawn Cemetary FM

(L) The Freemason Section of Forest Lawn Cemetery.
(R) Entrance to Forest Lawn.

By way of clarification, Babyland is the area in a cemetery named Forest Lawn where many of the children who were murdered found their final resting place, usually among the legitimate graves of other children. Forest Lawn Memorial Park cemetery is a five-minute drive from Hummel Park, and many of the satanic ceremonies that I remember happened in the chapel that is located on the grounds.

Interestingly enough, the chapel was built by Freemasons, and much of the cemetery is designed to be a celebratory resting place for the group, complete with a huge statue of an erected Freemason who overlooks the acres of members. Virtually every headstone has one or more of the symbols signifying the practice etched onto it, and though I am not sure how I feel about the group as a whole, I found the Freemasons' undeniable presence in a place where unspeakable atrocities occurred to be significant, but despite the controversy on the Freemason issue, Forest Lawn was nonetheless used as an incredibly efficient disposal system, as the dead were often simply cremated and disposed of. Underneath the chapel are rooms where the crematorium is located, which is also where games of "hide and seek" took place as well.

Chapel at Forest Lawn Cemetery.

On another note, after Gary Caradori's plane conveniently crashed near Robert Wadman's new jurisdiction in Illinois (enabling Wadman to be on the scene with no questions asked, even though he was one of the men Caradori was investigating), Wadman eventually sought employment in Wilmington, North Carolina, where he, once again a victim of coincidence, found himself ensnared by the same types of allegations that he experienced in Omaha concerning cult activity and child abuse—proof that a leopard doesn't change its spots.

Causing quite an uproar from what I understand, Wadman, as the only constant that connected the two situations, was either a victim of strangers conspiring against him, or he is guilty of the claims against him.

14

EVERYDAY LIFE IN WONDERLAND

t is easy to forget about God when you find yourself in the middle of hell, and I was no exception. Confused and struggling with who I was in relation to my past, I knew that I was changing, and not for the better.

I'd spent a great deal of my life denying everything that had happened to me and had become quite comfortable being considered "crazy," though Dr. Smith argued I was no such thing. However, the more I learned about Omaha and the people connected with its nefarious dealings, the more I realized that what I remembered was not only possible but probable, and worse yet, it hadn't gone away but had instead grown in complexity and scope—and not just in my head.

The issues I was unearthing were so dark that those around me began urging me to get out of all of it, especially after one afternoon when I received seventeen death threat calls on my answering machine. Message after message of nothing but the sound of a heart monitor bleep, the numbers registering on our caller ID showed us that the calls came from a local hospital. At first, we were convinced that our phone had gotten caught in some kind of computer loop, but after calling the hospital and being told that the number was one assigned for outgoing calls from room phones and pay phones, we realized that someone had been calling our house and intentionally leaving the messages.

I couldn't help feeling responsible for exposing the evil situations connected to my past, and that fighting this fight was somehow my destiny. This especially rang true when I discovered that one of the murdered boys in the 1980s in Omaha (none who were connected to John Joubert) vacationed with his family at the same lake in Minnesota on which my family had a trailer.

Much of what I knew concerning the case of abducted and murdered eleven-year-old Ricky Chadek seemed to point directly to my father and his friends. The fact that they allowed the bodies of Ricky and others to be found, despite the extremely efficient disposal system they had going, appeared to be some sort of message to someone, although what that was I didn't know.

Gangs often leave the dead as a message to others, and knowing the collection of men behind what was going on were similar, if not identical, to thugs on the street, separated not in deed but simply by money, I figured that the dead boy was a message to quiet someone.

When I mentioned how Gunderson's report on The Finders indicated a group of people profiting from abducting children, Sarah told me to look up the case of an abducted eleven-year-old in St. Joseph, Minnesota, on October 22, 1989. His name was Jacob Wetterling.

In two sketches of two different men, one of whom was believed to be the abductor, one of the pictures looked exactly like my father, while the other, although looking nothing like him, had on a hat that was an exact replica of the one my father always wore.

20 years before Amber, city grieved another child, May 28, 2006, *Omaha World-Herald* (page 1A): They were two Omaha children heading home as kids do all the time: a 12-year-old girl walking from a school bus stop, an 11-year-old boy pedaling his bicycle from a buddy's house. ... Shortly after Ricky Chadek disappeared, witnesses told police that an old blue truck with blue wooden sideboards had pulled into a parking lot behind him. Ricky was seen close to the truck. His mother found the bike in the lot. The circumstances screamed "abduction," investigators from the time said. ... Not quite eight days after Ricky disappeared, a farmer plowing a field spots something red in a ditch on the west side of 168th Street south of Ida Street.

Could DNA solve boy's 1986 death? March 25, 2011, *Omaha World-Herald* (p. 1B): New DNA evidence has helped Douglas County investigators eliminate some suspects in the 1986 killing of Ricky Chadek, one of the state's highest profile murder mysteries. ... Ricky, 11, disappeared from a bank parking lot near 42nd and Grover Streets on March 23, 1986.

New Leads in the Jacob Wetterling Abduction Case, March 1, 2011, KSTP-TV (Minneapolis): The Stearns County Sheriff says they have received 11 new leads in the disappearance of Jacob Wetterling, after the case was featured on a national news show Monday night.

The 21-year-old case was featured on CNN's *Nancy Grace* show ... Sheriff John Sanner says investigators are following up on the new leads, but could not elaborate to the extent of the tips. Jacob was 11 years old when he was abducted near his St. Joseph home on October 22nd, 1989. Police believe Jacob was abducted by a masked gunman, while biking home from a convenience store with his brother and a friend.

In July of 2010 investigators searched and seized items from a rural St. Joseph farm house. Investigators sent the items to the Bureau of Criminal Apprehension for testing. Results from the tests did not find any new substantial evidence in the case.

Sarah believed our father could be involved in the Wetterling abduction, and she told me that she'd followed the case from its beginnings, because she lived in the Minnesota area at the time, but she never knew whom to tell.

I called the National Center for Missing and Exploited Children and filed a report and then called the foundation the abducted boy's parents had created in his memory the next day. I told them what I suspected.

When a representative from the Jacob Wetterling Resource Center asked me which picture I believed was the abductor, I told the woman which one, following up by suggesting that the boy was abducted in a big blue truck—the utility truck my father drove all over the area as a Northern Propane gas man—which she confirmed was true.

I began sending out daily emails to everyone I could think of: media outlets, victim groups, anyone who might be able to help me. No one was willing to help; all I found around me were those people who wanted to silence me.

I was completely isolated in my search and spent most of my time interacting with the very worst society had to offer. Bombarded by chaos, I was becoming insolent and defensive, determined to get my father's activities investigated. I descended into a depression the likes of which I hadn't felt since I was a teenager.

In the midst of my investigation, dead animals began appearing out of nowhere in our front yard, our cars were vandalized, and

Ted Gunderson began to suggest that I was being intimidated with a nonlethal, anti-crowd microwave weapon. Having discovered that the weapons of which he spoke not only existed but that the Democratic National Convention had considered using them at their convention one year, I was no longer able to dismiss his claims, as crazy as they sounded.

The court case we had going against our stepmother to recover life insurance money had gone poorly, and both Sarah and I walked away feeling that we'd been duped. Sending us email after email, Shady explained to us that these things took time and that he was having problems with our stepmother's lawyer, who was, coincidentally, our stepmother's cousin.

At the end of our $5,000 retainer, Shady produced my father's "will," but although my father's name was signed at the bottom, the signature was in my stepmother's handwriting. Later, we both got a letter in the mail telling us that Shady's firm no longer represented us and that if we wished to pursue this case any further, we would have to go to court immediately as the statute of limitations was due to expire at the end of that year. Sarah and I both felt that Shady had played us.

Never having been able to force my father or his widow into court, I'd always hoped to be in front of a judge long enough to explain what I'm detailing in this book. Although I'd failed in that respect, I did succeed in what I had initially set out to do, as the fraudulent will was my proof that my father hadn't lied when he told me that he had included us as beneficiaries.

Years later, I saw Shady on a flight back from Chicago, and judging by his reaction, we were correct in assuming he'd swindled us. Neither of us said a word, but immediately after we latched eyes, his look became stricken. *DOC MARQUIS*

It wasn't just my father's family that went into attack mode but complete strangers as well, and not just in chat rooms but in real life. Soon after the death threats on my phone and dead animals in the yard, I was contacted via email and told that a man named Doc Marque wanted to speak with me. He lived in western Nebraska and had been involved with Satanism not as a victim but as a practitioner of the art, having written books detailing himself as an "Illuminati witch."

During our first and only conversation I realized that this man had written books about how he'd tortured people, including children, yet here he was, free as a bird, gay as Christmas, and eager to proudly declare how he'd hurt children. We spoke politely on the phone about my situation, despite the images in my mind of reaching through the phone and decking him.

My investigation was psychologically taxing, and eventually I found it impossible to sleep or keep grounded, even with Dr. Smith's help. Child abductions, ritual abuse, satanic churches, and Iran-Contra conspiracies, not to mention the death threats, were all difficult for her to believe.

People were shying away from me, no doubt uncomfortable with my constant anger, which would flare into rage at the slightest provocation. My voice, which is deep even in the best of times, had taken on stronger tones and inflections, and I knew that the intensity I was experiencing wasn't healthy. Dr. Smith assured me that it was a symptom of my childhood defense system while, during our sessions, she constantly tried to talk me down while patiently listening to my excuses as to why I found it impossible to control myself.

She observed that my anger was like being run over by an emotional freight train. Some sessions she just listened while I yelled about my frustration concerning the situations I was finding myself in and the fact that I, once again, felt powerless.

Everyone has a breaking point and mine came a year and a half into my investigation, when I had a "brief psychotic episode." Unable to sleep for two and a half weeks straight, I ended up going to my psychiatrist and begging her to admit me into a hospital. I'd spent the night before at Art's house in an attempt to try and sleep someplace else but couldn't.

He looked me straight in the eyes the next morning and told me that everyone was worried about me and that I needed help. He demanded that I drop the investigation, hugged me as I left to go home, and made me promise that I would seek help.

Delusional, confused, and desperate to sleep, I went to my psychiatrist's office right after and she committed me that morning. Believing I was safe and away from everything, the strange events of my present would follow me into the hospital regardless, when an implausible coincidence occurred.

BREAKDOWN

The weeks before my breakdown were awful. Tristan helplessly watched me descend into madness. Gunderson insisted that a microwave weapon was being used to inundate and silence me, possibly from as close as a neighbor's house, and all I knew was that I couldn't sleep and was losing the ability to determine what was real and what wasn't. I was unable to escape the growing paranoia that I was under attack.

Disheartened, I found myself in a mental hospital for the first time in my adult life. Drugs helped me sleep, and I began putting myself back together a couple days later, but having lost thirty pounds with huge black bags under my eyes, I had been shaken by the whole ordeal.

I was concerned that I was experiencing some sort of schizophrenia and maybe the staff thought so too. But the staff was incredulous when Tristan and Sarah assured them during a family therapy session that I was indeed pursuing an inquiry into satanic ritual abuse and government conspiracy. Sarah related a few of her own abuse experiences, and she and Tristan expressed their concerns, not that I was crazy but that what I was dealing with was so negative and destructive that they were afraid it would completely consume me.

Eventually with therapy, I determined that my focus should be on those who loved me rather than on a situation that seemed to have no foreseeable conclusion.

Everyone on the ward knew what I was dealing with, given that I'd spoken about it in group therapy. I'd become irritated with my doctor thinking I was "delusional" (at least before the family meeting), knowing I was correct about Omaha being a satanic ritual abuse capital. The staff, however, was skeptical and disbelieving.

All alone, I finally came to understand the childhood trauma that Sarah had come to terms with years before. I apologized for being so mean to her at the time she needed support the most, and I had begun to understand the resistance I'd felt for so many years whenever the past came up, as well as Sarah's determination not to get involved now. I was in over my head, I admitted, but it was when I decided to cut the strings that an implausible coincidence occurred.

A few days into my stay at the hospital, a woman was admitted with the last name *Gosch*. She introduced herself as Noreen Gosch's ex-husband's niece. I couldn't believe the coincidence, and though it seemed like a strange twist of fate, after what I'd just gone through, I couldn't help wondering if it was some sort of set-up.

Considering that I had been investigating the Gosch family and suddenly here was a member of the same family, who just happened to be in the same hospital at the same time as I, the hospital staff seemed to disregard the coincidence.

She told us that Johnny had indeed been a runaway, that he had lived with extreme physical abuse, contradicting everything his mother had purported. Talking over pizza, she told us about her family and why she felt that all situations concerning her cousin were a reflection of the craziness that was part of his mother's psychological makeup. Of course, what were the chances of running into such a person in such a place at such a time?

I was in the hospital for a week. The day I went home, I took down from the Web all of the videos and writings detailing my past. I felt disheartened by my failure but believed that those closest to me deserved my time and energy more than a situation way over my head and beyond my ability to resolve.

Finally, sleep came. But during my waking hours, I was overwhelmed with a debilitating depression. I sank deeper and deeper into despair, feeling as if I'd been abandoned by God. I spent hours crying, convinced that my failure was unforgiveable. Over-identifying with all the victims involved, my father who had wanted to come clean, not to mention my siblings and me, I felt as if I had let everyone down.

Concerned, Dr. Smith called my psychiatrist and asked that I be readmitted to the hospital. My church friend Susan felt that I was under spiritual attack, given that she too had had her own childhood experiences with Omaha, and she urged me to begin my spiritual practice again while Art counseled me to return to a church of some sort.

No longer isolated like I was the first time in the hospital, I reached out to friends and family and finally got a handle on my depression with the help of antidepressants. Nothing weird happened the second time I was hospitalized, and I was lucky enough to have my own personal psychiatrist work with me, which made all the difference in the world. However, following Susan's advice, I took a shamanic journey shortly after getting out of the hospital.

RISING ABOVE WONDERLAND

Raised as I was, I have always been aware that human beings are moving toward something spiritual, and because I believed in the satanic version of Christian "last days" Tribulation, it was easy for me to see a takeover by a rich and powerful group. Good at compartmentalizing my thoughts and emotions, I do it instinctively, as it was how I was taught to survive. However, I had begun to admit that I was no longer afraid that I was a bad guy and had actually started to see myself as Dr. Smith saw me: a normal human being who has had some incredibly abnormal experiences.

After getting out of the hospital the second time, I'd come to accept that life was rarely fair, but although there may not have been much justice on this side for the children I'd been fighting for, spiritually I had experienced a karmic sense of balance on the other side. Needing to know where he ended up, I did a journey in order to find out about Alan Baer.

During the shamanic journey, I found myself on top of a mountain confronted by the most mesmerizing blackness I had ever seen. Hypnotic, this *living darkness* was calling to me in a way impossible to resist, and had God not turned me from its gaze, instructing me never to return to this place, I might have been claimed that day. A black hole of spiritual nothingness, its call was impossible to resist, and I knew that this darkness was claiming those who have chosen to share its nature the minute they exhale their last breath. Coming face to face with *true* darkness, those involved with past events will find themselves on that mountaintop and be taken as Alan was taken.

After leaving that place, I was given a bird's-eye view of people I'd known and what had happened to them once they'd crossed over in death. Powerful and hedonistic in life, they had been consumed by their own hellish desires while still alive. My mother had endured years of physical torture, in and out of the hospital; my father, surrounded by ghouls waiting anxiously for him to die so they could materially benefit from his death; Alan, who had died from the inside out with people calling after his death to tell his widow how happy they were he was dead; Kevin Dobson living out his last days as a quadriplegic. Many of them had already "got theirs."

I recognized that God's justice is in many ways more exacting *and more exact* than anyone on earth could devise. When I had become so depressed that I had to return to the hospital that second time, I couldn't resign myself to the fact that, on this side, evil generally wins and good has little power over events. I'd been so obsessed with bringing justice to the front steps of the guilty, I never once considered that it might not be my place to do so.

Although I had discovered that my place in the scheme of things hadn't been the one I thought, as I was only one person and no man is an island, as the poet John Donne wrote, the important part for me was that I nonetheless had a place, and it was reclaiming this big picture perspective that helped me to regain my faith along with the balance I lacked for living life.

I returned home to Tristan and my studio, I returned to my artwork and spent the following year trying to forget the events that had led to my breakdown. I processed the past and tried to make sense of it.

15

EXPOSING SATAN

On Friday the thirteenth in March 2009, Yahoo ran a pop article about some of the history behind Friday the thirteenth. At the bottom of the article was a link to another pop article at LiveScience.com entitled "Top Ten Conspiracy Theories" by Benjamin Radford, managing editor of *Skeptical Inquirer* magazine.

Among the top ten conspiracy theories, satanic cults were number nine—itself a number favored by satanists and occultists of various persuasions. The article quoted Phillip Stevens, Jr., associate professor of anthropology at the State University of New York at Buffalo, who claimed that the satanic cults in the 1980s and early 1990s "constitute the greatest hoax perpetrated upon the American people in the twentieth century." Radford then adds that no proof of satanic activity has ever been shown, his evidence being the sensationalist claims of people like talk show host Geraldo Rivera.

Rivera's October 22, 1988, show "Devil Worship: Exposing Satan's Underground" ended up being nothing more than bad journalism convincing Americans that satanic ritual abuse was a hoax. Not the first time Rivera flopped, it however lacked the originality of his show two years earlier when he broke into Al Capone's empty vault on live national TV.

Claiming there is no proof is inaccurate. The McMartin day care center in which 1,200 children from McMartin, along with several other day cares in the area (including a Long Beach Catholic church conveniently downplayed in the news), refuted claims the children had been victims of satanic ritual abuse.

The fact that no convictions stuck doesn't mean it was simply "satanic panic," considering that after the trial, forensic archeologists were given three days to excavate the area, at which time they found tunnels and rooms containing satanic relics. These were indication that the children had been telling the truth about the rites they had testified to. They exemplified the issues that the trial hadn't wanted to address, not to mention begging the question as to how and why these tunnels remained hidden until after the trial.

How did so many children, in different parts of the nation, come up with the same claims around the same time and, more importantly, for what purpose? Why would parents subject themselves and their children to public scorn? Blaming it on the therapists who reported the issues and claiming they were guilty of crafting an "elaborate hoax" to bring down a bunch of day cares makes no sense, especially when you consider that it happened before the Internet.

The False Memory Syndrome Foundation (FMSF) is invaluable when it comes to dismissing the possibility of satanic ritual abuse from the public mind. Of course, some of its early funding originated from the North American Man/Boy Love Association (NAMBLA), with founding FMSF members connected with the

NAMBLA board itself. Like they say on *South Park*, "Dudes, you have sex with children."

North American Man/Boy Love Association (NAMBLA)

The North American Man/Boy Love Association (NAMBLA) was formed in 1978 as a political, civil rights, and educational organization. It was inspired by the success of a campaign based in Boston's gay community to defend against a local witchhunt, according to the NAMBLA website (nambla.org).

The organization calls for fundamental reform of the laws regarding relations between youth and adults and promotes consensual, loving relationships between younger and older people.

The website provides this message: "We condemn sexual abuse and all forms of coercion. Freely-chosen relationships differ from unwanted sex. Present laws, which focus only on the age of the participants, ignore the quality of their relationships. We know that differences in age do not preclude mutual, loving interaction between persons. NAMBLA is strongly opposed to age-of-consent laws and all other restrictions which deny men and boys the full enjoyment of their bodies and control over their own lives."

Many FMSF theories presented in court cases as "expert testimony" for the defense have since been disproved, as studies have shown that drugging and traumatizing a child does affect the child's brain and its ability to remember exactly.

The involvement of the False Memory Syndrome Foundation should be suspect, not just because of NAMBLA's conflict of interest, but consider this. Why would such a group form in the first place? Why has it been necessary to spend so much time and money on something that has been deemed a hoax? Unless, of course, they know something the rest of us don't.

Most harmful to victims of ritual abuse and satanic ritual abuse is Kenneth Lanning's *FBI Report on Satanic Ritual Abuse*. Of course, taking the FBI seriously is suspect in itself, as is expecting the FBI to investigate itself, as in Lanning's report. Considering that the man wasn't even part of the FBI at the time, comparing his report to Noblitt and Perskin's *Ritual Abuse in the Twenty-first Century: Psychological, Forensic, Social, and Political Considerations,* I found that the issues are not as cut and dried as our government has tried to present.

Noblitt is a clinical psychologist and Director of the Center for Counseling and Psychological Services in Dallas, and Perskin Noblitt is the Executive Director of the International Council on Cultism and Ritual Trauma. Both are experts on what is actually a complex psychological issue, not satanic panic.

The National Center for Missing and Exploited Children has said that a child is abducted every forty-three seconds, meaning roughly 800,000 children a year, or eight million in a decade— numbers that were tabulated by our own Justice Department. Why don't we, as a nation, know more about this problem within our borders? Why do the media always associate human trafficking with third-world countries while downplaying our own numbers?

Knowing that there is a great deal of money to be made from human trafficking, and considering how much money was being made in Omaha in the 1980s, at a time when there were no computers, no Internet, no social media or watchdog websites, it is an indication that all of this was well funded and certainly well protected.

Something obviously happened, at least here in Omaha, and you only need to examine the history and follow the money to discover who was behind it. It is as Arthur Conan Doyle wrote: "When you have eliminated the impossible, whatever remains, however improbable, must be the truth."

MILLENNIAL REFLECTIONS

Any social worker can tell you that an abused child often becomes hypervigilant of his surroundings, and I think those involved in my satanic ritual abuse wanted to know what would happen if they took that abuse to an extreme.

The first and only time I ever met face to face with John DeCamp, he would give me the word I had been searching for. DeCamp, a Nebraska legislator, was heavily involved in investigating events in Omaha and had written a book detailing his experiences. During our one and only meeting he stared uncomfortably at the floor and suggested what they were trying to create was a group of "psychic warriors," trying to dismiss the idea even as he said it out loud. However, he was right—that is exactly what they were doing.

My life has been a series of levels that I have had to process before I could accept what I was dealing with. For years I dealt with memories of physical abuse, but it wasn't until my mom died that I was able to face the sexual abuse. Dealing with the sexual, it was only after my father and sister died that I could bring myself to face the satanic aspect, and even then my understanding was limited.

My father's skeletons had been connected to something so vast that knowing the scope of the abuse put me into the hospital, but in time, I had to accept that as well. This process of acceptance has been a constant since then.

It was when I started to grasp the concept that the mind control Aquino had taught me was not only real, but that he had been right in believing that it worked, and I began to realize that it was the lessons I learned as a child that helped save me as an adult. That realization became the complete game changer for me.

The fact is that Aquino and his friends are perfect examples that rituals are believed to work in greater ways than in just the indoctrination of its members. Why else would they be so secret? Dismissed in the same context that we dismiss the Freemason group, although they are the first, largest, and most secret group in American history, whose top echelon consists of the world's richest men, Temple of Set is not the only example validating the fact that our nation's rich and powerful believe in the power of ritualistic practice .

Unable to fall into the same category of conspiracy theory that the Freemasons are afforded, California's Bohemian Grove is a testament to the fact that our rich and powerful adhere to secretive ritualistic practice. A playground for the super-rich and powerful, its borders are protected as fiercely as is the secrecy of the rituals practiced within the compound.

Virtually invisible to the general population, its existence is nonetheless well established and is known to have housed virtually all of our presidents at one point or another, as well as many of our nation's leaders.

With regard to the history surrounding the Bohemian Grove, it has been suggested that governmental policy has often been determined during its annual celebration, which breaks treaties as well as totally disregarding the nation's Constitution and laws of the land.

Whatever the case, the practice of rituals is well known to occur here, and although they remain steadfastly secret, they have been dismissed as nothing more than frat-boy antics. Nixon once inferred that the place was too homosexual for him. No one really knows exactly what happens at this place, but the fact that it exists, and in pretty much complete secrecy, is undeniable.

Not to digress, however, my point is that I am far from the only person who believes in the power of ritual, and Aquino, satanic founder of Temple of Set, who is well known to have often been in attendance at the Bohemian Grove, as a past teacher of mine, definitely has an appreciation for the art. This is not a secret.

Many of today's Christians seem to be hell bent on literally interpreting the Bible, but rarely bother to consider the question as to whether demons actually exist. Comfortable keeping the thought ambiguous, they rarely consider the question, as it is believed that communing with such beings is impossible, although Jesus Christ preached otherwise.

Having been raised to believe, it still took time to admit that what had happened to me, both in my past as well as spiritually, had actually happened, and was real. Unable to dismiss my childhood any longer, it took even longer to reach a point where I was able to allow myself to contemplate the larger implications of my experiences and what they may have had on events surrounding me.

Aquino's school of witchcraft was no Hogwarts, and I was regarded as nothing more than a host. Opening me through trauma, teaching me abilities I may never have had otherwise, all this was done in preparation for an event they believed was in my future. They helped me to become hypervigilant in a way that allowed for a much stronger consciousness of my surroundings, yet it was their activities that forced me to focus on the world within. Forcing my mind to expand, I was given the ability to think in ways far outside of the box, and I thank my experiences in Satanism for leading the way to my shamanic practice.

A brilliant man, with strong convictions, Aquino can in no way be considered crazy, nor can any of his associates. However, although they learned how to strongly influence conscious choice, they were unsuccessful in eradicating it.

They opened Pandora's Box for me, but they never considered that I would take what they taught me as a child further than they could control as an adult, and working within the context of shamanism, I was thus able to transform myself from a host into a doorway.

I am convinced that we are in a period of great spiritual judgment, and that this tribulation is calling souls to awaken. Once using Burke's observation, "All that is necessary for the triumph of evil is that good men do nothing," as a mantra, I have come to appreciate the value in the phrase: *Let go and let God.* Although Aquino and his associates were right about many things, they were wrong about one, however.

Always given a choice how we live our lives, we will either move toward a new world or thrust ourselves further into the palpable darkness that lies between this world and the other, a fact none of us, regardless of how rich or powerful we may be, can escape.

16

A MESSAGE TO SURVIVORS

B ecause of the torture we underwent as children—whether under the CIA's Artichoke/ MK-ULTRA program, ritual abuse, or satanic ritual abuse—we were broken in ways we will never get back.

I am well into my forties now, and I still grapple with residual fear and paranoia. I spent a good deal of my life hiding. When I wasn't hiding, I was running, most of all from myself. Having tried everything possible to escape the memories of what happened to the child I once was, there comes a time when a person can no longer run from the darkness that surrounds and permeates them, and I finally reached that point.

To ascend to heaven, one must first descend into hell to name the demons and lay them to rest. The story of Jesus Christ teaches us this. With the help of a fantastic therapist, I gleaned what I could from what had happened to me in order to escape the continual hell I was unconsciously creating for myself.

The most important thing to remember when working to release ourselves from shackles of childhood is that *the past is the past*. And regarding MK-ULTRA, ritual abuse, and satanic ritual abuse, it is crucial to know that they only picked the brightest to go through their training and programming. Sadly, many children did not survive, but many of us did. Bright enough to adapt to everything they threw at us, our survival is a testament to the brilliance residing within us. This is fundamental.

When I looked back, I understood that in many ways I was smarter than my handlers/trainers. The horrors they put us through were designed to stimulate the dormant part of the brain that would lead to psychic abilities and in so doing they taught us to do things that they themselves remain incapable of doing. We can look within and trust our intuition with that *knowing* side inside of us. They opened a part of our minds that they couldn't control, a part that gets stronger as we mature. When we finally make our past conscious, we are enabled to draw from the wisdom and use it.

Their most effective tool was fear. They taught us to be afraid of everything and everyone and not to trust. However, controlling a person with fear rarely works forever, and the more one tries to dominate with such tactics, the more the human spirit resists. Inevitably the victims start to feel contempt for the perpetrators. Contempt breeds anger, anger feeds thoughts of rebellion, and eventually all heaven breaks loose.

Given that what we experienced was internal and mental, we must remind ourselves that the revolution we're involved in is a *mind* revolution, while we learn to fight the urge to turn the fight onto ourselves, instead focusing it outward where it can still do some good.

In the past, there has been nowhere to go and no one has been willing to listen. Not able to really focus what we had experienced in any way that could make a difference, we've been shunned, ridiculed, dismissed, and ultimately ignored by most of society who have been hoodwinked by the media into believing that our government couldn't possibly be guilty of such things and taught that such memories are a "conspiracy theory."

History, however, is cyclic, and has a way of returning like a dog to its vomit. We find ourselves in the era of Guantánamo Bay and Abu Ghraib and Bagram. We must also admit that we are no longer children, and, more importantly, we have a voice. More importantly, for many of us, the talents they strove to elicit in us have grown in sophistication, and now, as adults, we are not only able to recover, but many of us have a passion to help others. I feel that, knowing what we do, it is thus our responsibility to prevent similar torture from happening to others.

Occasionally, Sarah and I talk about our past. She is still bothered by how only a campaign of silence greeted her when she came out and began talking about childhood memories, while a decade later, my experience has been completely different. My memories validated in a way I couldn't deny, and I think that is the biggest difference between us. We live in different times, and everything has changed in just a few years.

Historically, when the world has been presented with a new idea, the new perspective is always first ridiculed, and then resisted, until it is finally accepted. Galileo and Newton are examples of this process, considering that the people once believed the sun revolved around the earth and fought the concept of gravity with ferocity. In the third stage now, our experiences are about to become common knowledge, and accepted as fact.

As for what to do, first, reach out and educate yourself. Satanists and occultists believe that knowledge is power (*Scientia est potentia*)—and in this they are right. Putting fear aside, we are able to free ourselves when we accept that the things we remember are not only possible but probable. Understanding that there are others, many others, in the same boat helps; for me, it was a saving grace to know I wasn't alone. Sarah and Tristan were always there for me, but it took me a while to grasp the sheer *numbers* who had survived and are surviving the same experiences we did.

Second, although we were intimidated at a young age not to use it, we now have a voice, and it is the strongest and most powerful gift given us in this life. Every one of us has a story to tell, and every one of our stories is important, whatever the details. Simply standing up and saying, "This happened to me," sends ripples of truth throughout the world, and there is no better way to start reclaiming your power.

Last and probably most important, practice what they taught you. Look within; don't be afraid to find unusual answers. Our lessons may have been horrible, but we now have the choice to overcome the fear and allow ourselves to embrace what they taught us. This time, we have the power. What they forced open within us is awakening on its own merit, and we as a group are starting to become aware of not only our abilities as individuals but also our strength in numbers.

Our handlers' biggest weapon was to convince us that we were alone in the dark, helpless to stop what was happening to us. Those days are over and we are now in a time in which the world needs what we have learned. Owing it to ourselves, to others, and to God, we need to let ourselves shine in the way we were taught to do, finally practicing what we *taught ourselves* to do.

All of us survived because they couldn't break our light-bearer spirit. In darkness as children, we were forced to seek the light—something they couldn't stop, and it is this that binds us together and gives us a commonality with each other. Instead of embracing the dark, we became light bearers, discovering the *true* power within, and it is now time to let our collective light shine. Trust me: we are already shining. In fact, the light's so bright that when I look at it as a whole, it hurts my eyes.

America was a very different place thirty-plus years ago, when Omaha was a small town striving to be a big city. There were no cell phones, and the personal computers owned by a few were still clunky and awkward. In other words, we couldn't access information like we routinely do now, and we depended on the corporate media at the time to inform us of current events. Given that many of the owners of those media outlets were some of the very men engaged in profiting from drugs, arms, and child trafficking in and through Omaha, one can guess that there was a serious conflict of interest concerning the facts being presented for public consumption.

Thirty years ago, Omaha was pretty much a cow town, filled with small-town people trying to make a living in the "big" city at the center of the nation. In no way accustomed to the activities that came to light in the 1980s, Omaha residents had no choice but to take what the local media was presenting about investigations into the failed credit union, child trafficking, and activities surrounding several local wealthy businessmen accused of being involved—even the police chief.

Eventually, the national media got involved and headlined that things happening in Omaha led straight to the White House. In fact, events in Omaha were well connected and heavily funded by the first Bush presidency and the ex-head of the CIA's many government and business cronies. Local media, run or influenced by the very people accused of being involved, vehemently fought these revelations, calling them "witch hunts" and the reports of serious abuse against children "conspiracy theories."

Historically speaking, the rich have always done what they wanted. Very few of us will ever know what it is like to have the power to acquire anything we desire or do what we want when we want with no legal consequences. Only a select few ever truly understand the absolute power of having enough wealth to control their community, the legal system, media, and elected politicians. Lord Acton who said in 1887, "Power tends to corrupt, and absolute power corrupts absolutely," also said, "Great men are almost always bad men."

Fortunes were made from Omaha to Washington, D.C., in the 1980s, thanks to child trafficking and the cocaine pouring in from the Contras, yet local and national media did a fine job of covering up the truth that the rich got richer from crimes that most of us who believe in decency cannot even fathom.

Enamored by wealth and with those who have it, Americans have a tendency to accept inappropriate behaviors of the rich. Omaha media outlets run by men engaged in pedophilia and child snuff films distracted the public mind from hundreds of child abuse cases by either sensationalizing scapegoats or making those accused of such activities seem to be the victims (as when police chief Robert Wadman was "victimized" by Alicia Owen's "perjury"). Smoke and mirrors, bread and circuses have worked since the invention of the printing press as ways to distract the public from truths their elite masters do not want them to know.

Omaha is a glaring example of the evil that can be perpetrated on the unaware by the rich and powerful. In time, the truth generally breaks out, but how much is lost until it does? Events in

1980s Omaha have now been properly documented and exposed in books such as Nick Bryant's 2009 *The Franklin Scandal* and documentaries like *Conspiracy of Silence* (on YouTube) plus my own videos on YouTube and my website: DavidShurter.com.

To understand the underbelly of present day human trafficking with its staggering numbers—100,000 American children are forced into prostitution each year in the U.S.—just study Omaha in the 1980s, an American experimental lab for this deplorable global practice. Study how child crimes fell between the cracks of justice and were kept hidden for a generation. Can we learn how to stop such blatant misuses of power so that at least the histories of child abuse and human trafficking might not circle around to another era? It remains to be seen.

EPILOGUE

Having been a victim, I look upon myself now as a survivor. I've lived so many lives and had so many experiences that I sometimes feel very old.

In retrospect, it's funny how when you get on the right track, things just seem to fall into place. A year ago, I started writing this memoir in order to try to understand my experiences, which started me on the path of redemption in a way. Not intending to publish it, I wrote it simply to see it in black and white.

In August 2010, I attended a conference organized by SMART—Stop Mind Control and Ritual Abuse Today—concerning ritual abuse, mind control, and government abuses and torture. The conference coordinator, Neil Brick, is also a ritual abuse survivor who has developed a website (ritualabuse. us) detailing the existence of ritual abuse and the events currently surrounding many cases of such abuse.

The conference changed my life. It was in meeting so many people who had experienced the same things I had as a child that I discovered true camaraderie. Reminding myself that the reason I became involved with all of this in the first place was to help others heal, I gained a new perspective and strong sense of hope from meeting others who were fighting the same fight and making a difference.

Sarah and I have become incredibly close since our family members have died, given that it is just the two of us now. Our stepmother still lives in town, but we never see her. I don't see myself leaving Omaha now. It is said that once you wear out a pair of shoes here, you are destined to keep returning, and honestly Omaha is my home. All of our friends and family live here, and neither Tristan nor I wish to move away from our support group. Besides, with all of the construction in the past decade, it is physically no longer the city I grew up in, helping to keep at bay bad memories of the past.

Since the conference, I've gotten together with survivors and survivor advocates, and we've begun to develop an outreach organization for survivors struggling to come to terms with what happened to them as children through education and advocacy. Forming the North American Truth and Reconciliation Coalition (NATRCoalition.org), some of us have now begun to group together in a way that is trying to empower people to come forth and recount their experiences so that the general population can understand what has happened in America regarding ritual abuse and satanic ritual abuse.

It was in writing the details of my experiences that I have finally succeeded in reclaiming my life and spirituality through Shamanism, which, in turn, has helped to focus me on helping others in their spiritual search.

With regard to Omaha, and the events surrounding the Franklin Credit Union, the last victim to come forward with allegations concerning what happened here in Omaha was a boy by the name of Brad Fuglei. A good student, well liked, and an activist in his school, he made a formal complaint against some of the people involved in his abuse to the Omaha Police Department. However, the next week he was found dead of an apparent suicide.

Publicly this was never well known and would have been completely forgotten had it not been for Omaha's Mayor, Jim Suttle. You see, his right-hand man, Matthew Samp, and the one who was instrumental in getting him elected also happened to be one of the men Brad made a complaint against. The story was barely mentioned in the news; nonetheless, it was explained since the boy was dead, the complaint was dropped, and the matter was quickly dismissed.

Adhering to the general rule concerning the situation, it is perhaps, once again, another coincidence, but there seems to be an awful lot of them.

> Member of Suttle's Administration Resigns after Accusations, June 1, 2009, KPTM-TV: Seven days before officially taking office, there's already a shake-up in major-elect Jim Suttle's staff. In the *Omaha World-Herald* on Sunday, they called out Matthew Samp, a member of major-elect Jim Suttle's administration, for allegedly having a sexual relationship with a then 14-year-old Brad Fuglei in 1998.

Human trafficking is still a problem obviously, and the more we learn how interconnected pedophile groups are, the more we see how vast this problem really is and how it has corrupted the heart of the nation. Books such as *A Crime So Monstrous: Face-to-Face with Modern-Day Slavery* by E. Benjamin Skinner explain in detail the mindset of ritual abuse that keeps sex slaves and domestic servants quiet about what is happening to them.

The more we learn about human trafficking, the more we understand how ritual abuse is used to keep victims silent and in their place. The more we learn about street gangs, the more equipped we become in understanding the dynamics of how such profiteering works.

The bottom line in Omaha with regard to drug and child trafficking was money, no different than anyplace else. The better we understand the issue of human trafficking and the money that is and has been made for decades on the practice, the more we begin to grasp how prevalent this issue is in the United States. Pedophile groups such as Dreamboard, who have been discovered to have been in existence for decades, show us that the human trafficking problem is not just a recent phenomenon, and the numbers from the Justice Department show that there is a problem.

Although America has ignored it, the so-called satanic panic was not some hoax, but rather a call for help from a group of people who were left in the dark after reaching out to alert the public to incredible abuses by our own government. Although a strong indicator of our nation's human trafficking problem, Omaha is far from alone in dealing with allegations of satanic abuse, as the documentation shows places such as Atlanta, Seattle, Michigan, and California have all experienced such problems. No longer able to be explained away as mere coincidence, satanic ritual abuse can no longer be ignored, as there is far too much information indicating otherwise.

At this point, I look forward to whatever happens. The future is unpredictable, but I have lived a very full life, and, in the end, it is the love we take with us that matters most. Blessed with so much love that I felt as if I had to give something back, what you have read is my attempt to do just that.

Lasting impressions last a lifetime, so if I could impress one last thing upon you, it would be my belief that we are engaged in a rebirth. I believe that everything that is dying around us is waking up in the New Earth that exists on a different level than the one we currently reside and, in many ways, is the paradise we've been searching for. Although the spiritual is invisible, this does not mean it is not real, and I believe that we're undergoing a spiritual transition the likes of which we have never seen.

Getting darker before it gets lighter, we will all end up making our choices, and though it won't be easy, I can promise those of you who choose the light will find the path enlightening as well as inspiring. As light bearers, we must answer this call as our very souls depend upon it. The trumpets have sounded, the seals have been broken, and the hourglass is about out, indication that it is our time to come out of the dark.

NOTES

STATISTICS ON MISSING CHILDREN AND HUMAN TRAFFICKING

If you add to the current statistics on child trafficking the fact that 2,185 children disappear each *day*, it does not take much thought to realize that this social problem will grow worse as world and domestic poverty increases. More and more money will be made in the sex trade off the backs of millions of undocumented people. In fact, human trafficking may be one of the reasons that immigration reform constantly stalls out, as the drug trade and human trafficking is making some people very rich. Surely those involved in this global criminal industry have not overlooked the money that could be made off the large numbers of undocumented poor.

Considering that it takes a village to raise a child, and we are all children of God, we must educate ourselves about the interlinking of human trafficking and child abuse that is robbing hundreds of thousands of women and children of their most basic human birthright. Turning a blind eye to this mess will only allow it to fester and grow, not to mention that doing so is morally, ethically, and spiritually wrong. Here are a few sobering statistics minus the personal stories that lie behind them:

- Each year, an estimated 600,000 to 800,000 men, women, and children are trafficked across international borders (some international and non-governmental organizations place the number far higher), and the trade is growing (U.S. Department of State, Trafficking in Persons Report. Washington, D.C., 2004).

- Of the 600,000–800,000 people trafficked across international borders each year, 70 percent are female and 50 percent are children. The majority of these victims are forced into the commercial sex trade (U.S. Department of State, Trafficking in Persons Report. Washington, D.C., 2004).

- Each year, an estimated 14,500 to 17,500 foreign nationals are trafficked into the United States. The number of U.S. citizens trafficked within the country each year is even higher, with an estimated 200,000 American children at risk for trafficking into the sex industry. (U.S. Department of Justice, Report to Congress from Attorney General John Ashcroft on U.S. Government Efforts to Combat Trafficking in Persons in Fiscal Year 2003. Washington, D.C., 2004).

- The largest number of people trafficked into the United States come from East Asia and the Pacific (5,000 to 7,000 victims). The next highest numbers come from Latin America, Europe, and Eurasia, with between 3,500 to 5,500 victims from each (U.S. Department of Justice, Health & Human Services, State, Labor,

Homeland Security, Agriculture, and the U.S. Agency
for International Development. Assessment of the
U.S. Government Activities to Combat Trafficking in
Persons. Washington, D.C., 2004).

From National Center for Missing and Exploited Children at
Missingkids.com: Andrea J. Sedlak, David Finkelhor, Heather
Hammer, and Dana J. Schultz. U.S. Department of Justice.
"National Estimates of Missing Children: An Overview" in
*National Incidence Studies of Missing, Abducted, Runaway,
and Throwaway Children.* Washington, D.C.: Office of Juvenile
Justice and Delinquency Prevention, Office of Justice Programs,
U.S. Department of Justice, October 2002, page 5.

The U.S. Department of Justice also reports:

- 797,500 children (younger than eighteen) were reported
  missing in a one-year period of time studied resulting
  in an average of 2,185 children being reported missing
  each day.

- 203,900 children were victims of family abductions.

- 58,200 children were victims of non-family abductions.

- 115 children were victims of "stereotypical" kidnapping.
  (These crimes involve someone the child does not know
  or someone of slight acquaintance who holds the child
  overnight, transports the child fifty miles or more, kills
  the child, demands ransom, or intends to keep the child
  permanently.)

A SATANIC FAIRYTALE

The particular Satanism I was raised with was apocalyptic in nature and grounded in ancient beliefs of myth and prophecy, many of which are pagan and Gnostic in origin. All of it was grounded in a Judeo-Christian language.

To understand the theology of Satanism, you have to go back long before Jesus Christ, when *mythos* was just as important as *logos*. Back when intellectual mystics, later referred to as Gnostics, under the influence of Jewish, Egyptian, and Greek mythology, developed convictions concerning the fall from Eden and beginnings of humankind that can't accord with evolutionary biology. Later considered heretics by the Roman Catholic Church, these Gnostics believed that the true sin in the Garden of Eden didn't lie in eating from the Tree of the Knowledge of Good and Evil but rather with a God who envied man's new-found knowledge; that humankind's problems began not with the serpent, who revealed wisdom and knowledge, but instead was the fault of a jealous and vindictive God, who cast man and angel alike out of paradise in a tantrum; selfishly preventing man from eating from the Tree of Life as well.

As a child, I was told that there were two Gods: the God of Israel, God of the Old Testament considered the God of history, transcendent and "unknown" to man—ineffective, envious, and tyrannical. Then there was the God of humankind, ruler of the world, defender of personal choice, and generally considered to be the serpent in most Christian texts. (Yes, you read that correctly.)

Way back in history, God's female counterpart was devoutly worshipped. The Hebrew tribe knew her as Ashera, the wife of God. Egyptians knew her as Isis, the Greeks as Sophia or

274

Wisdom. Regardless of the name, this female aspect of God represented a special knowledge residing within, which can only be discovered in stages, a process the Greeks referred to as *gnosis*. Often worshipped in rituals involving sex, the Sophia aspect of *gnosis* was seen as holding the keys to life and death.

I was told that the Archangel Uriel guarded the gates to the Garden of Eden. Referred to as the Flame of God, Uriel was the angel of Divine Presence, archangel of salvation, keeper of Eden. Uriel recognized the power of life residing in Eve, and believing in free will and free choice, revealed to her the secrets of good and evil by allowing her to eat from the tree that provided the knowledge of good and evil. As a result, Uriel was banished from Eden by the jealous God and handed the book of Hades that forbade him to enter Heaven until every soul in the world had been tested.

All that subsequently happened to humankind resulted from this event. Wanting to return to Heaven, Uriel had sex with Eve and produced Cain, bestowing upon him godlike abilities. Later, to subjugate Eve and the divine power of the deep feminine within her and thus keep her secret knowledge (*gnosis*) from humankind, Sophia sent seven angels to rape Eve and produce Abel. All this was fueled by the tyrannical God jealous of the relationship between His two creations, man and angels. The goal was to eradicate the consequences of the hidden secret knowledge now at humankind's disposal.

Secret knowledge is very important to satanists, who believe the answers to life and death are found in the occult (hidden knowledge). As they see it, salvation (perfect *gnosis*) comes from experiencing all manner of sin. Libertine behavior acted out in rituals includes invoking certain angels, who in turn offer their services and protection. Satanists believe the commandments of the Creator God reflect ill will and envy, and that those who follow His laws do so out of bondage, duped by His promises that only end in death.

Rituals rotate around these premises. For example, disembowelment reflects the truth that humankind is the progeny of the serpent and is done to offer a special reverence to the hidden parent residing in the shape of a snake within us all. Although disembowelment rarely kills the victim immediately, as a child listening to the screams I always wished it would.

To be sacrificed in a satanic eucharist is considered an honor, a blessing that frees innocents from their bonds of life and sends them back to their Creator. Bathed and well-fed days before their deaths, they are exposed to the best life has to offer. But since the Creator decided long ago that life should be pain, God's favorites are delivered back to Him with a message as to how bad that pain can be. During rituals, emotional outbursts are not tolerated. Tears are viewed as a sign of weakness and dealt with ferociously. Self-control (dissociation) is always expected.

The Creator is not viewed as omnipotent or omniscient (Note: he had to ask Adam where he was after he ate from the apple of the Tree of the Knowledge of Good and Evil). Thus it is easy to see why satanists believe in the power of Uriel—Angel of Repentance, Bringer of the Cataclysm, Angel of Prophecy—and other earth-bound angels, who, with satanists' help, will one day be strong enough to rule over Heaven.

For their devotion, satanists are rewarded with unimaginable power and riches, as has been true for generations. Considering the social status that each satanist outside the coven held, I believed this to be true. As my father's son, and the next vessel that Uriel would inhabit, I would take my place as An~~~ the war with Heaven in the days of the Tribulation, whic~~~ occur in my adulthood.

Many satanic prophecies depend upon the constellation Ophiuchus, the Serpent Bearer, as it will reveal when the gates of Heaven open once more. Ophiuchus began with the Egyptian Goddess Isis aka Sophia, female counterpart of the Creator God, mother of Creation. Through history, Isis has changed many times, until—due to persecution by male-dominated religious sects that displace all femininity—she morphed into the male healer Asclepius. *Centaur*

Believers of this religion hold that Asclepius, raised by Chiron the centaur, eventually became the constellation Ophiuchus. Symbolic of mystic healing, it stands as the tenth sign in an astrological chart of 13 and is the most feminine of all the signs. In between Sagittarius and Scorpio, the Serpent Bearer touches the tip of the Sagittarius spear and stands upon the scorpion's stinger, while holding a snake that represents eternal life. Mayan calculations used a very similar astrological chart, as did the mystic Nostradamus, as well as the Chinese.

In classic mythology, Zeus killed Asclepius with a lightning bolt because of his power to heal, taught to him by the Centaur, which threatened Pluto's reign in Hades, thus safeguarding the key to man's immortality (a secret prize that satanists believe will be theirs when Heaven is overthrown).

Later, Zeus resurrected Asclepius by placing him and the Serpent (symbol of renewed life) among the stars. Today, Ophiuchus stands with the Serpent power between Sagittarius the Centaur, the mentor who taught him healing, and Scorpio whose occult stinger he stands on and controls. I was taught that Ophiuchus's heart is astrologically in the exact middle of the universe, where the gates of Heaven are located, and that a planetary alignment was going to occur in my adult life that would signal the ushering in of the coming Antichrist. Because it is directly in the middle of the Milky Way, I would learn as an adult that this planetary alignment was spot on and scientific fact.

Just as the Mayan calendar and Nostradamus predicted, so the satanists I grew up with believed we are in days of upheaval. Sometime before 2012, the Earth will align with the rest of the solar system within the heart of Ophiuchus in the middle of the Milky Way. Whether this time is also that which ushers in the Antichrist, at which time Uriel will usurp the Archangel Michael's power, remains to be seen, but as a child I was assured that this would be the case.

Of course, knowing what I do now, as an adult, I know this isn't going to happen. But this philosophy was strong within the concepts of my own reality and had a definite impact on me throughout my life.

REFERENCES

Bower, Tom. *The Paperclip Conspiracy: The Hunt for the Nazi Scientists.* New York: Little, Brown, 1987.

Bryant, Nick. *The Franklin Scandal: A Story of Powerbrokers, Child Abuse & Betrayal.* Walterville, Oregon: Trine Day, 2009.

Conspiracy of Silence. Documentary produced by Yorkshire Television, 1994.

DeCamp, John. *The Franklin Cover-Up: Child Abuse, Satanism, and Murder in Nebraska.* Lincoln, Neb.: AWT, Inc., 1992 (second edition revised 1996).

Foster, Stephen. *The Project MKULTRA Compendium: The CIA's Program of Research in Behavioral Modification.* Lulu, 2009.

Gosch, Noreen N. *Why Johnny Can't Come Home.* West Des Moines, Iowa: Johnny Gosch Foundation, 2000.

Gunderson, Ted. *The Finders Report.* Privately published report given to the author of this book by Gunderson.

Hamer, Bob. *The Last Undercover: The True Story of an FBI Agent's Dangerous Dance with Evil.* New York: Center Street, 2008.

Lanning, Kenneth. *FBI Report on Satanic Ritual Abuse.* All Nations Publishing, 2011.

Lichtblau, Eric. "Nazis Were Given 'Safe Haven' in U.S., Report Says," *The New York Times.* November 13, 2010, nytimes.com/2010/11/14/us/14nazis.html.

Mindell, Arnold. *Quantum Mind: The Edge Between Physics and Psychology.* Portland: Lao Tse Press, 2000.

Nathan, Debbie. *Sybil Exposed: The Extraordinary Story Behind the Famous Multiple Personality Case.* New York: Free Press, 2011.

Noblitt, James Randall and Pamela Sue Perskin. *Cult and Ritual Abuse: Its History, Anthropology, and Recent Discovery in Contemporary America.* Westport, Conn.: Praeger, 2000.

Noblitt, Randy and Pamela Perskin Noblitt. Eds. *Ritual Abuse in the Twenty-first Century: Psychological, Forensic, Social, and Political Considerations.* Bandon, Oregon: Robert Reed Publishers, 2008.

The North American Truth and Reconciliation Coalition (NATRC) NATRCoalition.org

Omaha World-Herald archives, Omaha.com.

Radford, Benjamin, LiveScience's Bad Science columnist and managing editor of *Skeptical Inquirer* magazine. "Top

Ten Conspiracy Theories." May 19, 2008, livescience.com/strangenews/top10-conspiracy-theories.html.

Shurter, David. The author has an ongoing blog and YouTube videos that include the documentary *Conspiracy of Silence* on his website at DavidShurter.com.

Skinner, E. Benjamin. *A Crime So Monstrous: Face-to-Face with Modern-Day Slavery*. Free Press, 2009.

SMART (Stop Mind Control and Ritual Abuse Today) at ritualabuse.us.

Steffon, Father Jeffrey. *Satanism: Is It Real?* Ann Arbor, Mich.: Servant Publications, 1992.

United States of America, Appellee, v. Gilberto Montoya, Appellant, United States Court of Appeals, Eighth Circuit, submitted Aug. 26, 1991. Decided Dec. 26, 1991 (952 F.2d 226).

North American Truth and Reconciliation Coalition Mission Statement

The North American Truth and Reconciliation Coalition (NATRC) seeks to raise public awareness about historical and ongoing human rights violations in North America and works to establish an accurate and truthful historical record of such crimes, including human trafficking, organized ritual crime, child soldiering, mind control experimentation, and other forms of torture in both the private and public spheres.

To find out more about NATRC, please go to
NATRCoalition.org.

If you or someone you know is being abused, please call 911.

ACKNOWLEDGMENTS

bove all, I thank the Mother and Father and the entire Universe for guiding and protecting me on my journey this time around. Without your love and light, my life would be bereft of pleasure, and I am thankful I was never abandoned.

I thank Dr. Noblitt, not only for writing the Foreword to this book, but also for his and his wife's relentless pursuit of the truth and healing for all abuse survivors everywhere. Their work has been instrumental in my healing, and I can't thank them enough for that.

Where would I be without my therapist "Dr. Smith" who helped me face that which I was always afraid to face: myself. I would not be the person I am today without her teachings and insights, and I owe her more than I could ever offer back.

"Tristan," you saved me in every way another person can save another. You, my dear, are my soul mate, and I love you more than I could ever express in words. Your courage to face my darkness and not run away is something that has forever changed me.

To Elana, Mary, Alex, and my advisers who worked behind the scenes—without all of you, *Rabbit Hole* would have never come to be. Your guidance and patience have been amazing, and all of you helped to make this book what it is in a way that I could never have achieved by myself. Thank you for believing in me and this work and for the absolute love you showed this work in its development.

I also want to thank the North American Truth and Reconciliation Coalition known as NATRC. I am proud to be working side by side with such an amazing group of people. Readers are urged to learn more at NATRCoalition.org and perhaps get involved in a movement that has developed throughout the years to shine light on human rights abuses.

I could not have done this book without the help and love of my wonderful sister "Sarah." I could never have done what I have if you had not blazed the path first.

Last but certainly never least, I thank all of you who have loved me throughout the years as I have grown and changed into the person I am today. Shelly Harder, Tracy Kristensen, Fred Baker, Jeffery Boe, Kat Gaul, and too many others to name—you guys make my days complete, and I would be lost without your friendship.

I am the luckiest man I know.

Made in the USA
Lexington, KY
14 May 2012